How Your Child Learns—
and Succeeds!

TWO BESTSELLING WORKS
COMPLETE IN ONE VOLUME

Cynthia Ulrich Tobias

GALAHAD BOOKS
NEW YORK

CONTENTS

the way they learn

Dedication

To my parents, Robert and Minnie Ulrich,
who have always believed the best of me;
my husband, John, who is my staunchest supporter;
and my twin sons, Michael and Robert,
who daily remind me that
there are truly no two alike!

Acknowledgments

*I would like to gratefully acknowledge my family,
friends, and colleagues who keep me richly supplied with
examples, anecdotes, and encouragement. I would also like
to express appreciation to my editor, Gwen Weising, for her
patience and wise guidance throughout this project. And I
especially want to thank Dr. James Dobson and all the
Focus on the Family staff. It is an organization that truly
makes me feel as though I'm home.*

Table of Contents

Chapter One

What Is a Learning Style?

"Here comes the first one!"

The atmosphere in the delivery room was charged with excitement and anticipation. It was a planned C-section, so I was fully awake to witness the arrival of our two sons that April afternoon.

The doctor held up a tiny red baby and whispered, "He's beautiful!" Two minutes later, the doctor held up another baby.

"He looks just like the first one!" a nurse cried.

I recognized them both immediately. On arrival, each boy already seemed to exhibit many of the same behaviors he had demonstrated during the last several months in the womb. The boys and I had started the process of getting to know one another almost from conception, and now I was amazed to see how different these two "identical" babies were from each other. While it will take years to become familiar with each boy's complex nature, their differences were evident from the very beginning.

Friends and acquaintances, gazing at the redheads, often ask "How do you tell them apart?" My standard reply: "Just watch them for a minute—you'll know." If you listen to the way they speak to each other and to you, if you watch the way they interact with people and situations, you will have little doubt that these boys, who share the same birthday, are very much individuals.

When they were still very small, a favorite toy for the twins was a small workbench with hammer and pegs. Robert, our go-for-the-gusto son, took great pleasure in vigorously pounding the pegs. Michael, more analytic by nature, was fascinated by the fact that in the middle of the workbench was a hole just the right size for storing the hammer.

If you are a parent with more than one child, you've already discovered that even children growing up in very similar circumstances and environments can have dramatically *dissimilar* approaches to life. You begin to realize that people are *fundamentally* different. The individual bents that cause each person to be unique, often bring an overwhelming challenge to parents. It is not enough to simply decide how children should be reared and then apply the same techniques to each child. Parents need to get to *know* their children, and *no two will be the same!*

Often, with the very best of intentions, we set out to chart the course and plan the events of our children's lives according to what makes sense to *us*— the way we did it. After all, we are living proof of what works! But what seldom occurs to us is that other people, perhaps even those in our own family, may view the world in an entirely different way than we do. It therefore stands to reason that when we try to teach or communicate with our children and others, they are not all going to benefit from the same approach.

If you're like many busy parents, you may become frustrated when you try to help your child follow directions, do homework, or review for a test. You may be convinced that your child simply isn't *trying* hard enough. The fact is, each of our children perceives the world differently from the way we do. Each child is a unique individual with his or her own natural strengths and preferences. These individual gifts or bents are called *learning styles*.

Although we accept and even cherish each child's uniqueness, it's often difficult to work with the combined variations of all our children when we're also trying to juggle family schedules and the many demands of school and work.

Knowing I was to be the mother of twins, I did a lot of reading. One article had an excellent suggestion for *every* parent. The writer suggested taking at least 15 minutes a day to spend alone with each child. It recommended you choose a safe and fun play area and then let your child show you how he or she prefers to play and interact with you. Short of absolute necessity, you should make no corrections, suggestions, or negative comments. Simply enjoy being with your child. Give as many positive comments as possible, and make some mental notes as to how your child prefers doing things. If you do this consistently with your children, you will be amazed to see how easy it is to identify their different learning styles!

Getting to know each of our children as individuals is an exhausting but rewarding proposition. The busier and more complicated our lives become, the harder it is to remember that each person in our family has a unique and valuable contribution to make from his or her own perspective.

It is my intention to help you discover these different perspectives and to aid you in developing quick, practical ways of helping your child adapt his or her inborn strengths to the varied demands of learning, both in school and throughout the rest of life.

Parents rarely *intentionally* frustrate their children, but intentional or not, it happens. By reading *The Way They Learn*, you can learn to identify many areas of frustration and conflict that can be directly attributed to a mismatch of the child's learning style and the parent's. This is not a deliberate defiance of parental authority by the child. The challenge for parents is to find positive ways of building on their children's natural strengths without sacrificing desired bottom-line outcomes. Believe it or not, it *can* be done!

Another important task for parents is to help their children effectively work with a variety of teachers who will undoubtedly have a number of different teaching styles. After reading this book, you will have gathered some very positive information to share with your children's teachers. Having been a teacher myself, I can tell you that if you will approach both administrators and teachers from a positive perspective, you will be surprised at how open they are to learning about your children's individual styles.

When I first started teaching, I quickly realized that many of my students did not learn the way I did. However, I honestly thought it was just because they didn't know *how*. Surely, if I could teach them to learn *my* way, it would eventually make perfect sense to them.

As a new teacher, I was determined to keep my students excited about school. Since I assumed that they were a lot like me, I decided that boredom was their greatest enemy. I began a one-woman crusade to prevent boredom in my classroom.

The first day of school, after my students left, I rearranged the desks into a new, creative seating plan. I didn't post a formal seating chart, so I was not expecting some of the reactions I got the next day.

"Where do I sit?" several students asked.

"Sit anywhere!" I replied enthusiastically. "The desks make a butterfly today. See the wing tips?"

"Well, where do you *want* us to sit?" they asked uncertainly.

Now I was becoming a bit frustrated. "I don't *care*," I insisted, "just choose a part of the butterfly and enjoy a new seat!"

Now they were walking around the room, peering under the desks.

"Where's the seat I had yesterday?" one student muttered.

That day many of my students notched their desks so they could find the same one the next day. I soon realized that one person's boredom is another person's security. Although I was well-loved and respected for my concern and creativity as a teacher those first years, many students seemed to really struggle with some of my methods. When I later discovered learning styles, I began to accommodate the students many different ways of learning. It was a great relief to know that those students whose styles were so different from my own weren't deliberately trying to annoy me!

This book is just the tip of the iceberg about learning styles. In it, I have highlighted the most practical aspects of five leading research models on the subject. An annotated bibliography is included so that you can continue more in-depth reading or studying. I think you will find it fascinating. For far too long we have had writers and researchers putting people into tight little boxes. But because each person is so complex and unique, no one learning styles model can fully describe what a person *is*. As enlightening as each new chapter of information in this book may be, please remember: Each is only a *piece* of the puzzle. We can recognize and identify patterns of behavior and communication that will become keys for understanding and appreciating style differences. What we dare not do is insist that each person fit neatly into a category.

Even though you will find some potentially invaluable checklists and assessments throughout this book, you will also discover that identifying and understanding individual learning styles is an ongoing journey of observations and impressions. As you read through and begin to use these concepts, keep in mind the following general guidelines:

Observe

Observe patterns of behavior. When you or your child experiences success, what are the circumstances that brought about that success?

Listen

Listen to the way a person communicates. If you only talk to others the way you want them to talk to *you*, you may discover you're speaking a language that is foreign to them. Listening carefully can teach you how you need to talk to them.

Experiment

Experiment with what works and what doesn't. Keep an open mind and remember that even if an approach to learning does not make sense to you, it may work for your children. We do not all learn in the same way.

Focus

Focus on natural strengths, not weaknesses. Unfortunately, it's so much easier to pinpoint areas of weakness that need improvement than to bolster sources of strength. But you can't build much on weaknesses—strengths provide a much better foundation!

Learn

Learn more about learning styles in general. Pay close attention to your children's and your own learning styles in particular.

Everything you discover in this book is only part of the larger picture. There is much more to learn, and that is why I have included an extensive bibliography. While you are reading this book, look for additional pieces of your children's learning style puzzle. Resist the temptation to put labels on your children or anyone else. Don't box them into any one learning style.

Once you begin discovering your natural strengths as well as those of your children, you will probably be relieved to learn that much of their struggle and behavior has more to do with inherent style than with something you failed to do as a parent.

After receiving some learning styles training, one harried home-school mother seemed particularly relieved to find out her young son was "normal." She admitted it had been very difficult to work with him, especially when it came to teaching him music. "Now I understand why," she said. "When I tell him the stems on the notes must be straight, he makes them diagonal, and when I ask him to name the notes, he gives them names like 'Larry.' " This child was not being deliberately difficult. He did not have learning disabilities. He simply applied his own unique perspective to the learning task.

In a Nutshell

Learning how to recognize and appreciate learning styles can help you identify the natural strengths and tendencies each individual possesses. As you read the following chapters, you'll discover some very positive things about yourself as well as your loved ones. This book is only the first step in your odyssey. It usually takes from three to five years of learning about, observing, and using learning styles information before it becomes second nature. Be patient with yourself, and don't worry about trying to formally identify people according to a particular learning style label.

Dr. Holland London, a seasoned clergyman and powerful communicator, recently spoke at a gathering I attended. In his inimitable way, he spoke on a variety of subjects in a very short time with wit and wisdom. At one point he paused and leaned closer to the microphone. "People often ask me why I take so many detours when I speak. I just tell them it's because those I'm trying to reach don't live on the highway."

As a parent and an educator, I sat there thinking about how hard we try to get children to move onto the highway so that we don't have to put up with the inconvenience of detours.

Perhaps instead of spending so much time and effort trying to convince our children to move onto the path we've designed, we could encourage them to get to their destination by allowing them a few minor detours. Who knows? We may even discover some places *we'd* like to travel off the beaten path!

Chapter Two

What Style Are You?

Послушайте меня

*A Russian phrase meaning
"Listen to me!"*

If I spoke to you in Russian but you didn't know the Russian language, you wouldn't understand me. If I noticed your bewildered expression, I might slow down and repeat my Russian phrase more clearly and in a louder tone. But despite my best efforts, no matter how many times I repeated it, how well I articulated it, or how loudly I spoke it, as long as I continued to speak Russian, the chances are pretty remote that you would understand what I was saying.

How often have you heard yourself saying to your children: "How many times do I have to *tell* you this?" or "What did I just *say*? Didn't you hear what I *just said?*" The fact is, they probably did hear the words you said but didn't understand what you meant. Each of us takes in information in a different way, and because our learning styles are so diverse, we may as well be trying to communicate with each other in two languages.

Early in our relationship, my husband and I frequently struggled to get our point across to one another. One day in frustration he said, "I'm just talking to *you* the way I want you to talk to *me*." He paused and then added, "And I guess maybe you're doing the same thing."

For the first time, we both realized that the golden rule, "Do unto others as you'd have them do unto you," doesn't always work when trying to communicate. If we only talk to people in the way we prefer they talk back to us, and they are busy doing the same thing, chances are good that no one is truly listening: We haven't reached a common level of communication.

THE GREGORC MODEL OF LEARNING STYLES

One of the most effective models for understanding learning style differences comes from the research of Dr. Anthony F. Gregorc. His model provides invaluable insights into how our minds perceive and understand information. Let's take a careful look at it.

Two Points of View

Perception: *The way we take in information.*

We know people are not all alike. What we don't always realize is that each of us tends to view the world in a way that makes the most sense to us as individuals. The way in which we view the world is called our *perception*. Perceptions shape what we think, how we make decisions, and how we define what's important to us. Our individual perceptions also determine our natural learning strengths, or *learning styles*.

There are two perceptual qualities that each mind possesses. They are **concrete** perception and **abstract** perception.

Concrete This quality lets us register information directly through our five senses: sight, smell, touch, taste, and hearing. When we are using our *concrete* abilities, we are dealing with what is here and now—the tangible, the obvious. We are not looking for hidden meanings or trying to make relationships between ideas or concepts. The key phrase simply stated is "**It is what it is.**"

Abstract

This quality allows us to visualize, to conceive ideas, to understand or believe what we can't actually see. When we are using this *abstract* quality, we are using our intuition, our intellect, our imagination: We are looking beyond what *is* to the more subtle implications. The key phrase for the abstract is "**It's not always what it seems.**"

Although everyone uses *both* concrete and abstract perceptual abilities every day, each person is more *comfortable* using one over the other. This becomes his or her dominant ability. For example, the person whose natural strength is *concrete* may prefer to listen in a direct, literal, no-nonsense manner. The person whose natural strength is *abstract* may often pick up the more subtle cues from others as they communicate.

My husband was driving on a busy Los Angeles freeway when I noticed a unique billboard and said to him, "John, look at that billboard!" John turned and looked. He looked and looked, and pretty soon we were driving into someone else's lane of traffic. Horns were honking; people were shouting.

I turned to him. "John, watch where you're driving, for heaven's sake!"

He replied calmly, "Cindy, you told me to *look* at the billboard. Did you mean *glance?*"

I was exasperated. "Wouldn't you *assume* that?"

He shook his head. "I assume nothing. You said look and I looked. The billboard hadn't done anything yet, and you didn't tell me what to look *for.*"

John, using concrete perceptions, took what I said at face value. It never occurred to me that he would take it quite so literally. It takes the abstract perceptual ability to "read between the lines."

Using What We Know

Ordering: *The way we use the information we perceive.*

Once we've taken the information in, we all use two methods of ordering what we know. According to Gregorc, the two ordering abilities are **sequential** and **random**.

Sequential

A sequential method of ordering allows our minds to organize information in a linear, step-by-step manner. When using *sequential* ability, we are following a logical train of thought, a conventional approach to dealing with information. Those who have strong sequential ordering abilities may prefer to have a plan and follow it, rather than relying on impulse. Their key phrase is **"Follow the steps."**

Random

Random ordering lets our minds organize information by chunks and with no particular sequence. When we are using our *random* ability, we may often be able to skip steps in a procedure and still produce the desired result. We might even start in the middle or begin at the end and work backwards. Those with a strong random way of ordering information may seem impulsive or more spontaneous. It appears as if they do not *have* a plan. Their key phrase is **"Just get it done!"**

Learning Styles

The way in which we view the world is called our . . .

Perception

We perceive in two ways . . .

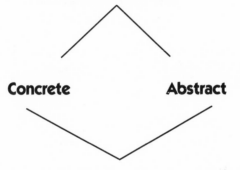

Concrete   **Abstract**

The way we use the information we perceive is called . . .

Ordering

We order in two ways . . .

Sequential   **Random**

At a recent training workshop attended primarily by accountants and data processors, the participants were asked how many balanced their checkbooks monthly. The majority, of course, were very careful to balance to the penny.

One man raised his hand and said, "I took the checkbook away from my wife." As the group frowned, he quickly explained. "We have checks that are a series of pictures. My wife was giving her checks out according to which *picture* she thought the person would like best. She thought as long as all the numbers were used, it wouldn't matter whether or not they were in order. So, she'd be at a fish market and say, 'Wait a minute, I think I have a picture of a fish on one of these!' "

What was considered essential to this detail-oriented, sequential accountant hadn't even occurred to his random-oriented wife.

Four Combinations

When we take all of Gregorc's definitions and put them together, we get four combinations of the strongest perceptual and ordering abilities. Remember, no individual is only *one* style. Each of us has a dominant style or styles that give us a unique blend of natural strengths and abilities.

From perception and ordering come four dominant learning styles. The following charts list some words most often used to describe those who are dominant in each style.

Four Combinations

Concrete Sequential (CS)

hardworking

conventional

accurate

stable

dependable

consistent

factual

organized

Abstract Sequential (AS)

analytic

objective

knowledgeable

thorough

structured

logical

deliberate

systematic

Abstract Random (AR)

sensitive

compassionate

perceptive

imaginative

idealistic

sentimental

spontaneous

flexible

Concrete Random (CR)

quick

intuitive

curious

realistic

creative

innovative

instinctive

adventurous

By learning some of the common characteristics of each of these combinations (**CS, AS, AR, CR**), we can recognize and value what we like to do best and what comes naturally for us. We can also learn to identify and improve characteristics that we avoid because we do not understand them well.

We, as parents, must first recognize our *own* natural learning styles. As we recognize how *we* learn new information, we can better understand what comes naturally to us and to our children, and can identify the differences between parents and children that cause frustration and misunderstanding.

The following checklist is a quick, informal method of identifying some of our own learning style characteristics. If you would like to do a formal assessment of your style, you will want to order *The Gregorc Adult Style Delineator*,[1] available directly from Dr. Gregorc. Once again, keep in mind that all of us are combinations of these four learning styles. No person will fit neatly into any one category.

Dominant Learning Style Characteristics

Describe what you prefer *most of the time*. Place a check mark beside every phrase under each section that describes your preferences. Check as many as you feel *strongly* describe you.

Dominant Concrete Sequential (CS)

I almost *always*:

___prefer doing things the same way

___work best with people who won't hesitate to take immediate action

___am more interested in obvious facts than in finding hidden meanings

___prefer a neat and orderly environment

___ask first "How do I do it?"

Total:____

Dominant Abstract Sequential (AS)

I almost *always*:

___want as much information as possible before making a decision

___need enough time to do a thorough job

___prefer to get directions in writing

___am interested in where a person got the facts

___ask "Where do I find more information?"

Total:____

Dominant Abstract Random (AR)

I almost *always*:

___prefer to check with others before making final decisions

___try to be sensitive to other people's feelings

___work well with others

___am not bothered by a cluttered environment

___ask the advice of others when in doubt

Total:____

Dominant Concrete Random (CR)

I almost *always*:

___solve problems creatively

___act on the spur of the moment

___work best with those who can keep up

___like frequent changes in the environment

___prefer to learn only what's necessary to know

Total:____

Based on the work of Anthony F. Gregorc, Ph.D. Adapted by Cynthia Ulrich Tobias, M.Ed.
(Do not reproduce without written permission)

Now that you have an idea what your dominant learning style might be, here's a quick overview and comparison of the four styles on some key issues.

What Do They Do Best?

Dominant Concrete Sequential (CS)
Their Key Word: *Facts*

- apply ideas in a practical way
- organize
- fine-tune ideas to make them more efficient, economical, etc.
- produce concrete products from abstract ideas
- work well within time limits

Dominant Abstract Sequential (AS)
Their Key Words: *Underlying Principles*

- gather data before making decisions
- analyze ideas
- research
- provide logical sequence
- use facts to prove or disprove theories
- analyze the means to achieve a goal

Dominant Abstract Random (AR)
Their Key Words: *Personal Relevance*

- listen sincerely to others
- understand feelings and emotions
- focus on themes and ideas
- bring harmony to group situations
- have good rapport with almost anybody
- recognize the emotional needs of others

Dominant Concrete Random (CR)
Their Key Words: *Compelling Reasons*

- inspire others to take action
- see many options and solutions
- contribute unusual and creative ideas
- visualize the future
- often find a different way to do things
- accept many types of people
- think fast on their feet
- take risks

What Makes the Most Sense to Them?

Dominant Concrete Sequential (CS)

- working systematically, step by step
- paying close attention to details
- having a schedule to follow
- using literal interpretations
- knowing what's expected of them
- establishing routines, and ways of doing things

Dominant Abstract Sequential (AS)

- using exact, well-researched information
- learning more by watching than doing
- using logical reasoning
- needing a teacher who is an expert on the subject
- living in the world of abstract ideas
- working through an issue thoroughly

Dominant Abstract Random (AR)

- personalizing learning
- having broad, general principles
- maintaining friendly relationships with everyone whenever possible
- participating enthusiastically in projects they believe in
- emphasizing high morale
- deciding with the heart, not the head

Dominant Concrete Random (CR)

- using insight and instinct to solve problems
- working with general time frames rather than specific deadlines
- developing and testing many solutions
- using real-life experiences to learn
- trying something themselves rather than taking your word for it

What's Hard For Them?

Dominant Concrete Sequential (CS)

- working in groups
- discussion with no specific point
- working in an disorganized environment
- following incomplete or unclear directions
- working with abstract ideas
- demands to "use your imagination"
- questions with no right or wrong answers

Dominant Abstract Sequential (AS)

- no time to deal with a subject thoroughly
- repeating the same tasks over
- lots of specific rules and regulations
- "sentimental" thinking
- expressing their emotions
- being diplomatic when convincing someone else of their point of view
- not monopolizing a conversation about a subject that interests them

Dominant Abstract Random (AR)

- having to explain or justify feelings
- competition
- working with unfriendly people
- giving exact details
- accepting even positive criticism
- focusing on one thing at a time

Dominant Concrete Random (CR)

- restrictions and limitations
- formal reports
- routines
- re-doing anything once it's done
- keeping detailed records
- showing how they got an answer
- choosing only one answer
- having no options

What Questions Do They Ask When Learning?

Dominant Concrete Sequential (CS)

- What facts do I need?
- How do I do it?
- What should it look like?
- When is it due?

Dominant Abstract Sequential (AS)

- How do I know this is true?
- Have we considered all the possibilities?
- What will we need to accomplish this?

Dominant Abstract Random (AR)

- What does this have to do with me?
- How can I make a difference?

Dominant Concrete Random (CR)

- How much of this is really necessary?

In a Nutshell

Just because your children aren't responding to you doesn't always mean they aren't listening. It could be that the difference in your perspectives is so great that you sometimes might as well be living in different countries and speaking different languages. Learning to listen to *how* something is said instead of just the *words* that are said can help everyone communicate more effectively. It can literally make a world of difference!

Chapter Three

The Dominant
Concrete Sequential (CS)
Learning Style

It was board meeting night for the local church. For some reason, those who attended that particular meeting preferred a more random style of learning and communicating. Missing from the meeting were the Concrete Sequentials, those who approach tasks in a step-by-step manner. Since there was a quorum, the randoms decided to go ahead with the meeting.

The main item on the agenda was promotion of the upcoming rally. "Hey!" someone said excitedly, "I've got a great idea!" (A phrase, by the way, that strikes dread into most CS hearts!) "What if we bought 1,000 balloons and filled them with helium? We could put a notice about the rally inside each balloon and release them into the sky. They would come down all over the area, and people would find out about the event." All the other randoms thought that was a wonderful idea, and later that week one of them went out and bought the balloons.

Before the actual launching of the event, however, there was one more board meeting and the CS members showed up that night. The randoms enthusiastically shared their plan, and the CSs politely listened. At the end, one CS raised his hand. "Do you know how far helium balloons *go* before they come down?" he asked.

The randoms looked a bit uncomfortable. "Well, no," one admitted. The CS replied, "They've been known to go as far as 200 or 300 miles. I don't think people on the other side of the mountains will come."

"Oh, yeah, we didn't think of that," a random said.

Another CS raised her hand. "Do you know how *long* helium balloons stay in the air before they come down?" she inquired.

"No." A random admitted, now a bit sheepish.

She continued. "They've been known to stay up as long as two or three months. The rally will be over."

And the randoms said quietly, "Oh, yeah, you're right."

The box of 1,000 balloons still sits, unused, under an office desk. But the board members learned a valuable lesson. In times past, the randoms had sometimes thought that the CSs were just shooting down good ideas and critically picking apart visionary plans. Now they realized that the CSs' contributions were invaluable. These days at that church's board meetings, it's not unusual to hear someone say: "Wait! We can't start without the CSs!"

THE DOMINANT CONCRETE SEQUENTIAL ADULT

When presented with an abstract idea, Concrete Sequentials have a special talent for seeing the practical side of an issue. They have a knack for knowing how to get the most productive use out of any item or plan—for streamlining and making everything work more efficiently. Their natural ability to think in a linear manner makes them people who can actually put together those "ready-to-assemble" products by following the step-by-step instructions.

A CS lives life in a fairly straightforward manner. Verbal communication sometimes comes across as clipped and bossy. The CS attitude is "If it needs to be done, you do it," and "If it needs to be said, you say it." The CSs are no-nonsense communicators, saying what they mean and meaning what they say. They don't usually pick up on subtle clues or hidden meanings. They prefer you tell them exactly what it is you want them to do.

Although my husband is dominantly Abstract Sequential, he is also very CS. I learned long ago that when he uses his CS style, he needs more than hints to fulfill my wish list for gifts on special occasions. On our first Christmas together, he really built up his "big gift" to me. "It's red," he said, "something you'd never buy for yourself, and it's too big to fit under the tree." On Christmas Day, I found my gift sitting in the carport. It was a bright, shiny red . . . lawnmower! After a few more Christmases of receiving jumper cables, blenders, and shower curtains, I finally came to grips with the fact that he could not read my mind. He would keep telling me that he truly wanted to make me happy—but I needed to *tell* him what would *make* me happy. Although he's getting better at remembering what I like, he's absolutely thrilled when I just make him a list of exactly what I want.

Giving practical gifts is only one way dominant CSs demonstrate their ability for being down-to-earth and realistic. Because of their hands-on sequential nature, CSs are very good at making and keeping schedules and organizing and maintaining systems. List-making comes naturally, and some extreme CSs even admit to being so dependent on a list that if they do something *not* on the list they *add* it so they can have the satisfaction of crossing it off. CSs are often the ones taking up the slack, picking up the pieces, cleaning up the messes, and putting away the leftovers. CSs would rather do it themselves than leave it undone, but if they do it, they do not suffer silently! Those who live with CSs may find notes reminding them of their responsibilities, or they may receive quick lectures designed to leave them feeling at least a *little* guilty.

THE DOMINANT CONCRETE SEQUENTIAL PARENT

The bleary-eyed couple was almost an hour late to the Saturday morning parenting workshop. The woman was very apologetic. "I'm afraid we overslept. We rented the three most *boring* movies last night," she explained. "It took us until almost 2 A.M. to finish watching them."

When I asked why they had subjected themselves to such an endlessly boring evening, she looked surprised. "Why, we *paid* to watch the movies. We *started* them. *We couldn't just quit in the middle!*"

Dominant CSs have a definite sense of order and responsibility, and they need to have a beginning, a middle, *and* an end. When dealing with their children, it is common for CS parents to:

- Communicate with their children in a literal, specific manner and expect the same in return.
- Believe that a yes or no question deserves a yes or no response, not a lengthy explanation.
- Expect instruction to be followed without question or procrastination.
- Clearly lay out the rules children are expected to follow, as well as the consequences for disobedience. Both are specific and consistent.
- Become frustrated when they have to say things more than once.
- Become exasperated at the child who seems to choose the "hard way" to do what the CS sees as a simple task.

CS parents almost always have high expectations when it comes to their children's behavior and academic success. After all, the CS parent probably had little trouble adapting to the traditional learning methods most schools use, since those methods tend to be concrete and sequential. If a child is struggling, the CS parent may often believe it is because that child is simply not trying hard enough.

CS parents are not likely to accept excuses like "It's too hard," "I don't like it," or "I just don't get it!" Part of the CS nature is to simply do what needs to be done, whether or not you *feel* like it. Duty and obligation play a big part in their own lives, and they expect their children to respond in the same way.

When it comes to discipline, the CS parent expects the child to do what he's told or suffer the consequences. In the CS parent's mind, the *threat* of punishment should be enough to prevent the bad behavior. When children don't do what they're told the first time, a favorite CS method for getting quick action is the "countdown."

Although the countdown works for many children, it does not work for all. For example, my mom would say to my sister, "Sandee, I want you here by the time I count to three! One . . . two . . . " and Sandee was *there*.

I, on the other hand, was not so compliant. My strong-willed nature compelled me to ride out the threat. Mom would start counting. "One . . . two . . . two-and-a-half . . . two-and-three-quarters . . . two-and-seven-eighths. . . ." I often called her bluff, just to see what would happen. Inevitably, I would experience the consequences!

Here is another classic example of style contrast. A CS parent frowns disapprovingly at the strong-willed, Concrete Random child who is contemplating standing on the coffee table and warns, "If you stand on that table, I'll spank you." The CR child pauses a moment, then shrugs and says, "OK, go ahead and spank me. How hard could it be? How long could it last? It's worth it."

To CS parents, the mere threat of a spanking would have been sufficient. It's hard for them to understand a child who would rather be punished than be pressured into obeying.

On the other hand, for a CS child, the CS parent's methods and approach make sense almost automatically. After all, they understand how each other's minds work. The CS child finds it comforting to know what to expect, and there is a sense of security about the consistency of routine and schedule. For the more random child, however, the CS parent's approach often seems dictatorial and rigid. Because a random person's perspective is so drastically different from a sequential's, trying to understand each other's point of view may literally be like listening to a foreign language.

THE DOMINANT CONCRETE SEQUENTIAL CHILD

Kelli was a bright and conscientious third grader. The class that caused her the most difficulty was history. One evening she had just read the chapter on Georgia, and she was answering the questions at the end. The first question was "What are Savannah, Georgia's, natural resources?" Kelli was stumped. She reread the entire chapter but could not find those two words, *natural resources*. As she was becoming more and more frustrated, her dad sat down with her. "What's the problem, Kelli?" he asked.

"I can't find *natural resources* anywhere," Kelli sighed. Her dad then defined the term and gave her one or two examples. Suddenly, a light went on for Kelli. This time as she went back through the chapter, she quickly picked them out. Because of her dominant CS style, she had easily remembered specific details. However, she had to be taught to recognize abstract concepts. Like their parental counterparts, CS children are very good at dealing with facts, but they have to work at seeing the abstract, bigger picture.

Some common characteristics of Dominant Concrete Sequential children are:

- They are usually very organized, specific, and conscientious.
- They may ask repeatedly for clarification or more detailed instructions because of their need to be sure they are doing things right.
- They are almost always more secure when there is a pattern to follow, model to copy, or someone to go first and show them how it's done.
- In getting CS children to do their chores, learn responsibility, and practice acceptable behaviors, they respond best to tangible rewards and hands-on methods. Often a schedule or checklist on the refrigerator is a great motivator for young CS children. Stars, stickers, and even cash are all effective rewards for a job well done.
- Consistency is especially important, and CS children may frequently have to remind their more random parents of a promise or a missed step in the routine. It may not even occur to the random parent to *create* a checklist, much less keep it up to date!
- CS children will generally take parents at their word. Since CSs tend to be very literal in their communication, more abstract parents may find their instructions misunderstood because they assumed their CS children understood what was *meant*, not just what was *said*.

A young mother was concerned when her five-year-old daughter came home from the first day of kindergarten absolutely exhausted. "Why are you so tired?" Mom asked.

The new kindergartner replied breathlessly, "Oh, Mom, I practically *ran* all day long!"

"Why did you run so much?"

The child answered very seriously. "Well, the teacher said 'When you're on the sidewalk, *walk*; when you're on the grass, *run*.' I was on the grass a *lot*, so I just had to keep running." This mother got pretty clear signals about how strong the CS characteristics are in her child!

Ten-year-old Tracy is a very conscientious, literal CS child and has been from the very beginning. During a recent visit to a shopping mall, she asked a question that had evidently been on her mind for awhile. "Why do those big trash cans say 'THANK YOU' on the flap?"

Her mother patiently explained, "It's to thank people who put their trash in there."

Tracy nodded her understanding but persisted. "But not everyone *puts* their trash in there."

Her mother waved her hand in dismissal. "Well, it just thanks the people who do."

Tracy frowned and pronounced her CS opinion. "Then it should say, 'THANK YOU *IF* YOU PUT YOUR TRASH IN HERE.'"

Parents of children like Tracy can help their CS offspring capitalize on this gift for literal interpretation by first understanding for themselves and then pointing out to the child the benefits of being a CS. For example, CSs catch a lot of mistakes because they look at everything so literally! When CS children feel reassured about the value of their natural communication strengths, it becomes easier to encourage them to stretch and look *beyond* their style.

WHAT ABOUT STRESS?

When it comes to what causes and relieves stress, the dominant CS parents and children have a lot in common.

The Dominant Concrete Sequential usually thrives with

organization	predictability	schedules
routines	tangible rewards	literal language

The Dominant Concrete Sequential is often stressed by

too much to do	not knowing expectations
not knowing where to begin	vague or general directions
no clean, quiet places	not seeing an example

You can frequently lessen the stress by

giving specific time and space for quiet, uninterrupted work
asking what you can do to help
providing a concrete example of what is expected
practicing "what if" scenarios to prepare for the unexpected

CONCRETE SEQUENTIAL

What People with Other Styles Admire Most About CSs

organization
attention to detail
completion of tasks
productivity
stability and dependability

Negative Perception By People with Other Styles

perfectionists
things often seem more important than people
tunnel-vision
lack of adaptibility
impatient

Ten Commandments for Getting Along with a CS

Thou shalt:
be consistent
be organized
practice common sense
pull your own weight
remember I have feelings, too
give advance notice so I can prepare myself
follow instructions
tell me what you want
take responsibility for your actions
not deal in generalities

In a Nutshell

Dominant Concrete Sequentials contribute a great deal to their families and to society with their natural bent toward organization, predictability, literal communication, and the ability to follow and give step-by-step instructions. Their greatest creativity may show up when they are fine-tuning and improving someone else's original idea. They provide a stable, predictable backdrop in the lives of those who may not even realize how much they count on having them be there. Their consistency and reliability often make them more valuable than some randoms would like to admit. Remember that everyone has at least *some* of the CS learning style in them. Just because it's not your dominant style doesn't mean you can't use it at least briefly when you need to. The more you learn to recognize CS strengths, the more you will appreciate those who come by them naturally!

Chapter Four

The Dominant
Abstract Sequential (AS)
Learning Style

It was still early in their marriage when a young couple discovered they needed to replace one of their cars. The young wife, acting in her typically random fashion, said enthusiastically, "Let's go to the car lot and look around!" Her husband, a Dominant Abstract Sequential, looked at her incredulously. "We don't even know what we're *looking* for," he stated. She shrugged. "Won't we know when we see it?"

Three weeks later, after they had listed critical attributes, researched *Consumer Reports*, charted interest rates and lease options, and had driven the top 10 cars twice, she realized her car buying days would never be the same as they were before marriage. Although her AS husband took all the *romance* out of car shopping, they *did* make a significantly more economical choice. Now if he would just quit second-guessing himself on whether or not they had bought at exactly the right *time*!

THE DOMINANT ABSTRACT SEQUENTIAL ADULT

When it comes to making decisions, the dominantly AS person feels compelled to explore virtually all the options. As a matter of fact, the information-gathering process is so important to ASs, that they don't do much of *anything* without a great deal of deliberation and thought. ASs are gifted with a natural sense of logic and reason. They evaluate almost everything, from major life decisions and purchases to a simple lunch choice on a restaurant menu.

What is especially unique about the AS evaluation process is that the analysis does not stop even after the final decision has been made. Although the process is done less actively, ASs admit that they never really stop looking to make sure there isn't a better option.

If an item has already been purchased and the AS later finds a better deal, there are, for the AS, really only two choices. If it's not too late, the item is exchanged. If it *is* too late, ASs may kick themselves for years, and there's almost nothing you can do to lessen the remorse.

Even though this may sound extreme, I've been told by several ASs that their penchant for finding the absolute best bargain even extends to the gifts they receive. As they are opening their gifts, the most dominant of them can't resist calculating how they could get *twice* the merchandise for the exchange value of the gift if they just waited for the right sale.

Analysis comes naturally to ASs, and most believe there can *never* really be enough information. They seem to be on a continual search for knowledge. There aren't enough hours in each day for ASs to do the research they feel needs to be done.

Since most ASs assume that everyone has the same need they do for extensive information, you may frequently get very long answers to short questions. It's difficult for ASs not to monopolize the conversation when it's a topic that interests them. And even though you may be finished listening, they may not pick up on your impatience.

The need for analysis and objectivity carries over into the more personal aspects of the AS's life. Although ASs may experience as much emotion as the next person, they believe that their emotions should be justified by facts. For example, I'm told by many ASs that falling in love is a difficult situation when it comes to applying principles of logic and reason. Most ASs may revel in the euphoric emotion of love, but they rarely make a serious commitment until they are certain there are solid and reliable facts to back up their emotional involvement. ASs will rarely share what they are feeling until they have a handle on *why* they are feeling the way they do. By the same token, they expect you to be able to justify *your* emotions.

I learned some important lessons about ASs early in my relationship with the AS man who is now my husband. We had only been dating about three months when we had a pretty serious argument. I was so upset when we parted that I went right home and poured my jumbled thoughts out on paper, not sure if I actually dared to send the letter to John. After some soul searching, I went ahead and mailed it.

A day or so later, John called me, and asked if he could take me to lunch to discuss my letter. He picked me up, and while we were sitting in the car, he took out my heartfelt, soul-baring epistle. He had rewritten it in outline form—Roman numeral I, II, III; subhead A, B, C. I was too horrified to speak! He sensed my dismay and quickly explained. "Cindy, I love you. What you wrote obviously meant a lot to you. If I were to just answer you off the top of my head, I might well miss the points that were most important to you. So I put this in a format where I could be sure all your concerns were addressed."

How could I argue with that? His meticulous approach that at first seemed to be so cold and calculating was actually motivated by the same love and tenderness that had caused me to randomly spill my thoughts on paper.

THE DOMINANT ABSTRACT SEQUENTIAL PARENT

I'll never forget one morning when Robert, one of our 18-month-old sons, had been fussing and crying for hours, and we could find no solution for his tears. Finally in frustration, John said, "Rob! For heaven's sake, just *articulate* what it is you *want!*"

AS parents insist that their children demonstrate at least some semblance of logical thought and analysis. Because of a naturally intellectual bent, ASs sometimes forget they are dealing with young children and not their own peers. AS parents tend to have high expectations for their offspring. Remember, ASs believe in thorough deliberation and complete analysis of virtually every situation. A simple request from a child like "Could I have a puppy?" may very well bring about more trouble than that child thinks it's worth! The AS parent will likely respond with questions like, "What kind of puppy? Where will you keep it? What will you feed it? How will you keep it groomed? How much will the upkeep cost?" ASs may even require that their children keep detailed records or present a well-thought-out written request in the first place.

It is especially important to AS parents that their children learn to think logically. ASs feel compelled to look beyond the obvious and find the under-lying principle. It is this understanding of the "moral of the story" that often creates the need for an AS parent to be sure the child has "learned his lesson." ASs have a strong need for closure, and they often find themselves asking their child, "Now, what have you learned from this?" A child with a random style may create a great deal of frustration for the AS parent, because it seems almost impossible to direct that dominantly random mind into a structured analysis of circumstances or problems.

I recently heard an excellent suggestion from a visiting professor. She said her AS husband was very fond of lecturing their impatient and impetu-ous random teenage daughter. The girl hated the long, drawn out lectures, and her father was very annoyed by her apparent lack of attention. After several unsuccessful encounters, they came up with a unique agreement. When the father began his lecture, his daughter could stop him at any time during the lecture and state what she thought the point was that he was trying to make. If she got it right, he had to abort the rest of the lecture. If she missed the point he was allowed to continue until she hit upon the actual point he was making. Now he knew she was listening, and she knew she would not need to endure a prolonged explanation of a point he had already driven home.

This is the kind of compromise that can help AS parents come to terms with children who do not share their drive to analyze, verbalize, and philosophize.

THE DOMINANT ABSTRACT SEQUENTIAL CHILD

A frustrated home-school mom struggled with her AS first grader as she tried to teach him to read. Somehow Jimmy had gotten the idea that he should already *know* how to read. Because he felt he was starting at a disadvantage, he simply avoided his reading lessons altogether. After reading about learning styles and discovering that Jimmy's AS traits called for more distance and objectivity, his mother hit upon a unique solution. She took Jimmy to the store and told him he could choose any puppet that appealed to him. He selected Molasses the Moose. When they got the puppet home, mother and child began to teach Molasses to read. Now there was objective distance, and there was no longer a stigma in Jimmy's mind about learning the basics. This AS child rapidly learned while teaching Molasses, all the while making sure that his moose paid close attention and worked very diligently.

Dominant Abstract Sequential children are usually as systematic and deliberate as their parental counterparts. These children almost always need more time to complete tasks to their satisfaction. Although they may appear to be slow, it is often a case of being thorough. Parents of AS children express amazement when the child would rather not do an assignment or project at *all* if there is not time to do it *completely*. Frequently, AS children can have a homework assignment almost completely finished, but if told to "just turn in what you have," they will turn in nothing.

It is common for AS children to appear quieter and more withdrawn. Their minds are working through the analytic and evaluative process, and it's not likely they will verbalize what they are thinking until they understand it.

One extroverted mother became very worried about her uncommunicative AS daughter, Allison. The young girl would spend hours alone in her room, thinking and reading. She would rarely contribute verbally to family or classroom discussions. Allison's written assignments, however, were almost always superb. Allison's mother attended one of my workshops on learning styles and discovered her daughter's AS strengths. After coming to understand her daughter's approach, this normally outspoken mother was able to appreciate the depth of insight Allison possessed. Once she let her AS daughter work in solitude without pressure, she discovered Allison began to be more comfortable verbalizing how she felt.

AS children have a gift of objectivity that begins to show up at a very early age, and they are often uncomfortable with tasks or assignments that seem too personal. It is difficult for the AS to share emotions, especially if the emotions cannot be explained logically or categorized efficiently. Even "show and tell" at school can be painful if the AS is forced to reveal something that seems to intrude upon their privacy. Parents can often help their AS children deal with their discomfort if they encourage their AS child to analyze *why* this particular assignment is important.

WHAT ABOUT STRESS?

When it comes to what causes and relieves stress, the dominant AS parent and child have a lot in common.

The Dominant Abstract Sequential usually thrives with

organization	credible sources of information
logical outcomes	opportunities for analysis
plenty of time to work	appreciation for their input

The Dominant Abstract Sequential is often stressed by

being rushed through anything
unreasonable deadlines
not having hard questions answered
abiding by sentimental decisions
being asked to express emotions or feelings

You can frequently lessen the stress by

providing additional time to complete tasks
giving lots of space and quiet time to work
putting as much as possible in writing
appreciating the less emotional aspects of a situation

ABSTRACT SEQUENTIAL

What People with Other Styles Admire Most About ASs

analyze before making a decision
ability to conceptualize an idea
intellect
precision
ready knowledge

Negative Perceptions by People with Other Styles

aloofness
not in touch with reality
have to have an explanation for everything
highly opinionated
perceive things in numbers, not effort

Ten Commandments for Getting Along with an AS

Thou shalt:

have specific goals when dealing with me

use logic and reason

listen to what I have to say

give me a job, leave me alone, and let me do it

be complete and thorough

be deliberate

keep issues factual

give me time to research projects for the best approach

make certain I understand the purpose of the project

don't expect immediate response—I need time to think
     and research

In a Nutshell

The dominant AS learner is in the minority among the general popu-
lation. The views of the strong AS will not always make sense to or even
be welcomed by those who do not share the same devotion to logic and
objectivity. Although it may seem that the AS has an entirely too serious and methodical perspective on life, there is also a warm and loving
side that can sometimes be overlooked by those who don't recognize or
value the AS's approach. Once again, we all have at least a little of every
learning style. Even if your AS tendencies are virtually hidden, learning how to access this part of your style can definitely be a benefit!

Chapter Five

The Dominant
Abstract Random(AR)
Learning Style

The suspect in the crime sat alone in the interrogation room. Officer Baker, one of the department's best by-the-book cops, stormed out in frustration. "He won't talk! I tried every method we were ever taught, and the guy won't budge."

Detective Frye smiled and said, "Let me talk to him."

"I'm telling you," Baker said angrily, "I've tried it all."

Detective Frye had been in the room less than five minutes when Baker, watching the suspect through the one-way mirror, stared in disbelief. The suspect's head was in his hands, and he was sobbing. Detective Frye had turned on the recorder, and the full confession took less than an hour.

"What did you do?" Baker asked when Frye came out.

Detective Frye shrugged. "I just talked to him."

THE DOMINANT ABSTRACT RANDOM ADULT

During my time as a police officer, I noticed that dominant sequential detectives and police officers had a particularly frustrating time dealing with unpredictable or uncooperative people. In the police academy we were taught how to interrogate a suspect, interview a victim, and solicit information from a witness. There are certain procedures to follow. So, when a sequential officer follows procedure to the letter and those tried-and-true methods fail to work, he is often at a loss. That's what happened in the story above. Officer Baker, a CS, could not understand how Detective Frye, an Abstract Random could come over, speak a couple sentences, and cause the suspect to pour out his heart. In many cases, the technique simply isn't something one could learn from a book.

The AR has a sixth sense when it comes to reading people or understanding what others need without anyone verbalizing those needs aloud. Nonverbal cues that may completely escape the more sequential person can speak volumes to the AR.

Because ARs place so much trust in intuition, their instincts become more and more accurate over the years. Unfortunately, it does not seem to get any easier for ARs to explain *how* they know what they know if they did not use sequential abilities in arriving at conclusions.

The Dominant Abstract Random person believes there is more to life than cold hard facts or endless details. People are more important than things, and life is too short to get caught up in conflict or uncomfortable situations. They often find themselves the peacemakers, sometimes at their own expense. It is difficult for ARs to work in situations where there is unhappiness or disharmony. For many ARs, it seems as though they are constantly having to smooth over rough words said by someone else, or apologize for the actions of a thoughtless colleague or family member.

It is especially important for ARs to feel included. Before making a decision, they almost always seek the input of trusted friends and family. ARs are at their best when they are part of a team process. Soliciting opinions from those around them helps them maintain a cooperative life-style.

Although my dominant style is Concrete Random, my AR preferences are very strong. I noticed how heavily I relied on it early in my dating relationship with my very sequential husband. We experienced a conflict common to many couples.

John would ask, "Do you want to go out for dinner?"

"Yes," I would reply enthusiastically.

"Where would you like to go?" he would query.

Not wanting to make an unpopular choice, I would hedge. "I don't know, what do *you* feel like eating?"

He would shrug. "It doesn't matter. Just choose a restaurant."

Not actually *believing* that it didn't matter, I would keep after him until he became impatient with me. Why couldn't I just make a *decision?* I would feel hurt. Didn't he realize it was because I valued his opinion? Of course, by the time we finally *did* get to a restaurant, we were too irritated with each other to enjoy our dinner.

Eventually we both realized what the other one needed, so John then designed an almost foolproof method for avoiding the conflict. Now when the question of where to go for dinner comes up, he says: "Chinese, Mexican, or American?" He chooses three cuisines he would be equally happy eating.

"Chinese," I say.

He then suggests three Chinese restaurants he finds equally appealing. I choose one of those three, and we're off, usually in less than a minute. I get the necessary input, he gets a quick decision, and we both enjoy our evening!

What may sometimes seem to others to be a lack of conviction or inability to make up their minds, is often simply the ARs' efforts to make sure that everyone involved in the process gets what he or she needs. In reality, ARs often possess the strongest convictions of all, and once they have chosen a battlefield, no one is more committed to the end result.

THE ABSTRACT RANDOM PARENT

The room was happily chaotic, with piles of papers, crumpled food wrappers, and freshly laundered clothes waiting to be folded. Almost hidden on the desk was a lovingly framed sign declaring a cheerful, AR motto: A tidy house is the sign of a misspent life!

Although ARs can keep house as well as any sequential, housekeeping is not a high priority if there are personal needs to fulfill. By nature, ARs are somewhat unstructured and free-flowing, and they often struggle when it comes to keeping a consistent schedule or detailed routine. Dominantly AR parents are warm, nurturing, and full of praise and reassurance for their children. When it comes to dealing with a more sequential child, AR parents can be perceived as inconsistent, even though it may simply be a case of deciding what really needs to be an issue and what isn't all that important in the greater scheme of things.

The ARs insistence at avoiding conflict and confrontation can sometimes make them a target for being the "soft touch" in the family. In many cases, ARs would simply "rather switch than fight." They do strive to keep everyone happy, and that can mean giving in on issues that may have been firmly enforced by the more sequential parent. Although ARs will usually stand firmly for the nonnegotiable issues of physical safety and moral and ethical values, almost everything else is really dependent on the day and the mood of the AR. Unfortunately, this may send mixed messages, especially to a more sequential child. The child may get in trouble for doing something one day and the next day it goes by completely unnoticed.

AR parents married to more sequential spouses often find themselves in conflict over issues of disciplining the children. ARs may feel they need to bend over backwards to soften the methods of the sequential parent. And the sequential spouse may continually feel like "the bad guy," because he or she has to enforce a structure that the AR tends to avoid.

ARs are usually very conscientious parents, and they often feel badly that they are asking their children to be organized and keep rooms clean, when the AR parents themselves are hard-pressed to do the same. It is relatively easy to make ARs feel guilty. Early in their lives, children can pick up on this, and unfortunately can master the art of manipulating the AR parent. ARs are very sensitive to how others feel, and it is both an asset and a liability to care so much about what others think.

THE ABSTRACT RANDOM CHILD

One mother good-naturedly complained that when her Abstract Random daughter got a teacher she liked, it turned out to be quite expensive. "At least twice a week, my daughter would tell me we needed to buy or make something nice for Mrs. Hughes because she'd had a rough day." After a year of gifts and thank-you notes, Mom had a new appreciation for her daughter's thoughtfulness and sensitivity. "However, next year, we're hoping our daughter gets a teacher who's a little more even tempered!" the mother admitted.

The Dominant Abstract Random child, probably more than any of the other learning styles, cares about pleasing people. For the AR child, all of life and learning is an intensely personal experience.

It is difficult for ARs to concentrate on learning something that doesn't appear to have any effect on their own life or the lives of people who matter to them. ARs may be motivated to get good grades simply because it means so much to their parents. They may frequently be accused of "not living up to your potential" because they rarely pursue knowledge purely for the love of learning.

In the nursing program at a local university, administrators discovered they were losing a lot of potentially good nursing candidates. Upon closer examination, they found that many of the dropouts were AR students. The ARs were drawn to the profession out of a sense of personal nurturing and devotion to the well-being of others. Unfortunately, no one really warned them about all the very *un*-AR classes that must be endured before they could successfully fulfill their dream. The professors decided to stay close to the AR students and coach them by reminding them why they wanted to become nurses in the first place—to save lives and make a difference. Somehow it made the classes in physics, chemistry, and anatomy personal challenges that must be met to achieve the ultimate goal. Almost everyone discovered that the AR can ace the most difficult class as long as there is a personal, passionate commitment to the outcome.

The AR child may have a difficult time in a classroom where other children are not happy or where they feel the teacher does not take a personal interest in or liking to them. It's almost like the AR has invisible antenna up at all times, scanning the atmosphere for trouble spots. If there is conflict or strife between personalities, it is almost impossible for the AR to concentrate on learning.

It is almost always the AR child who will come up to the teacher and say something like, "Susie's dog got run over this morning, and she's crying. Could we go into the other room so I can talk to her?" The CS or AS children may *also* point out Susie's distress, but usually they will say something like, "Susie's crying. Do you think you could get someone to go talk to her?" It doesn't take long for the other children to realize that it is the AR who can most naturally listen to and comfort those in need.

WHAT ABOUT STRESS?

When it comes to what causes and relieves stress, the dominant AR parent and child have a lot in common.

The Dominant Abstract Random usually thrives with

> frequent, honest praise
> reassurance of love and worth
> opportunities to work together
> opportunities to use creativity and imagination
> acceptance of personal feelings and emotions

The Dominant Abstract Random is often stressed by

> having to justify feelings
> competing individually
> not feeling liked or appreciated
> pressure by loved ones to be more sequential

You can frequently lessen the stress by

> allowing the AR to work together with someone else
> noticing the good things without pointing out the bad
> daily reassurance of love and value to the family and the world
> just listening without offering unsolicited advice

ABSTRACT RANDOM

What People with Other Styles Admire Most

spontaneity

concern for others

sociability

adaptability

ability to understand
how others feel

Negative Perceptions by People with Other Styles

unpredictable

don't take a hard stand

overly sensitive to criticism

not aware of time limitations

smooth over problems rather than solve them

Ten Commandments for Getting Along with ARs

Thou shalt:

give me the opportunity to help others

give me feedback (positive/negative)—where do I stand?

not be so serious

not nit-pick

remember, I will get things done—even if it's not your way

not put me in the middle of a conflict

allow me to be spontaneous

show appreciation

not mistake a happy exterior for lack of intelligence

know that not all is written in stone

In a Nutshell

When it comes to being in touch with others, sensing what needs to be done, and getting along with difficult people, there don't seem to be any better candidates for sainthood than ARs. As one person put it, "When they gave out love and kindness, you ARs got double-dipped!" Other styles can sometimes sell the ARs short by not appreciating the spontaneity and flexibility that comes as part of the package. If we want to learn to get along with other people, each of us must daily use our AR skills.

Chapter Six

The Dominant
Concrete Random (CR)
Learning Style

The Concrete Sequential mom had just taken a big drink of juice when she made a horrible face and spit it out. "Ack! This tastes *awful*!" she said.

Her Concrete Random son reached for the glass. "Let me try it," he offered.

She looked at him as if he had lost his mind. "Don't you trust me?" she asked. "Why would you *want* to taste something I just told you was awful?"

It wasn't that her CR son didn't *trust* her—he just needed to *experience* facts in order to actually believe them.

THE DOMINANT CONCRETE RANDOM ADULT

The Dominant Concrete Random person is probably the least likely to take your word about anything. These people have a compelling need to experience as much for themselves as they possibly can. CRs, more than any other style, strive *not* to be ordinary. If you say that something is so for everyone, CRs will tell you that they are *not* everyone, so what is true for others is not necessarily true for them.

Because the CR lives in the "real world," usually anything that can't be experienced firsthand cannot be fully trusted. CRs are notorious risk takers. They believe you cannot break away from the ordinary unless you are willing to go out on a limb.

CRs are intuitive, quick-thinking, curious, and resourceful. The concrete part of their nature makes them very "hands-on," but their random ordering process causes them to be somewhat unpredictable. The CRs often fight structure and routine, preferring to keep all their options open. Life usually goes by at a breathless pace with CRs because they are constantly looking for new challenges and untried doors. If something becomes routine or boring, CRs simply drop it and go on to the next, more exciting prospect.

It's not unusual for CRs to have several careers in a lifetime, sometimes even two careers at once. It is not necessarily a lack of focus as much as a desire for variety, a sense of being able to conquer the unknown. The resourceful CR nature keenly grasps the obvious and can quickly turn it into something unexpected.

As I was driving home the other evening, I heard my two-and-a-half-year-old twin sons arguing in the back seat. Michael (CR extraordinaire) was hitting his AR brother, Robert. Although I suspected what was going on, I decided to give him the benefit of the doubt.

"Michael," I said sternly, "I'm pulling over and turning on the light. If you are hitting your brother, you are in big trouble." I stopped the car, switched on the light, and turned around to see Michael's hand resting on his brother's arm. With lightning-fast reflexes, Mike grinned at me and said, "*Tickle, tickle, tickle!*"

It was a perfect example of the CRs natural gift for getting in *and* out of trouble quickly. Because they can think so well on their feet, it is rare that you can catch them violating a given rule, even if they get off on a technicality.

CRs, for the most part, consider most rules to be simply guidelines. In their thinking, rules are for people who don't know how to do the right thing in the first place.

I am, admittedly, a strong CR. One year it was almost Christmas, and my AR sister Sandee, one of her small children, and I were Christmas shopping in a department store. When we got to the escalator with the stroller, Sandee noticed a sign that said, "No strollers allowed on the escalator." While she was reading the sign, I was busy loading the stroller onto the moving stairway.

Sandee was horrified. "The sign says no strollers on the escalator!" she cried.

I looked at her. "Oh, are the *stroller police* going to get us?" I asked sarcastically. "Sandee, this sign is for people who don't know how to safely put a stroller on an escalator. Since I *do* know how, it doesn't apply to me."

She refused to follow me upstairs for several minutes, not wanting anyone in the store to realize she was with someone who so blatantly disregarded a *rule*. For me, it was simply a *guideline*.

It is difficult for the CR to accept limits and restrictions, especially if the rules seem arbitrary or dictatorial. Most CRs believe in being law-abiding citizens and are especially conscious of setting a good example for their children. CRs have the most trouble with rules and regulations that do not seem to have practical reasons for their existence.

"Rank has its privileges" is *not* a CR motto, and "Just because I said so" is almost never accepted without challenge. The CR will not be deterred by the word *impossible* if he or she has determined the goal is a worthy one. At the other extreme, even the most accessible goal may be ignored by a CR who has decided achieving it is just not worth the trouble.

One young CR woman came up after a recent seminar and said, "I just have to tell you my own CR story!" She said that when she enrolled in a college chemistry class, she was surprised to hear the professor make a rather brash statement at the beginning of the first session. He told the students that since no one could possibly get an A on any test without doing the homework, the homework would count as 50 percent of the total semester grade.

This CR woman immediately bristled. *What did he mean it wasn't possible to get an A without doing the homework?* "Right then and there," she told me, "I decided I wasn't going to do a drop of homework. And I *did* get a A on every test."

I smiled at her and said, "But you got a C in the class, didn't you?"

She grinned. "Yep, but it was the best C I ever got!"

CRs sometimes frustrate people of more sequential styles because they don't go by the book, and they constantly seek to change the system or try something new. It is these very bents, however, that keep everyone growing and challenged to consider new and uncharted possibilities.

THE DOMINANT CONCRETE RANDOM PARENT

One evening, a young CR father read his four-year-old son, also a Concrete Random, a bedtime story and tucked him in. As the father left the room, the boy said, "Dad, leave the hall light on."

Dad replied, "No, son, we're not going to leave the hall light on."

"Yes, I want the hall light on."

"No, no hall light."

"Yes!"

"No!"

"Yes!"

"No!" And the hall light went off.

The boy started to cry. The parents decided he could jolly well cry himself to sleep. But two hours later, *everybody* was sick of it. The boy was tired of crying, but he wasn't going to give in. The parents were tired of listening to him, but it had been decided that the hall light was *not* going to go on.

Finally the father walked back down the hall, looked into the room, and discovered his son had uncovered one of his feet from the blanket. The teary-eyed little boy said, "Dad, if you'll cover my foot, I'll go to sleep."

So his dad covered his foot and the boy went to sleep. You see, the war was no longer worth winning—but for both CR parent and CR child, unconditional surrender was out of the question.

The father needed to maintain his authority as a parent, but his compromise allowed his CR son a graceful way to surrender the battle.

CR parents often find themselves frustrated by children who do not do what they are told. Now, mind you, CR parents would be the *last* to do something just because you said so. But once CRs have decided how something should be, they tend to issue ultimatums or orders that they themselves probably wouldn't obey.

CRs are passionate about their convictions. CR parents want the best for their children, but they can sometimes find themselves insisting that their children accept the CR way whether the children like it or not.

CRs often make fun and exciting playmates for their children, actively participating in almost everything and encouraging their children to play whatever game it is for all they're worth. Life for CRs is an adventure, and they will be the first to conquer uncharted territories and slay scary dragons.

Because CR parents understand the CR nature of their children, you would think they would get along well. Although they sometimes do, being alike is not always a benefit. Since the CR parent doesn't want to back down anymore than the CR child does, it often makes for an unflinching standoff between parent and child.

THE DOMINANT CONCRETE RANDOM CHILD

A kindergarten teacher gave her class a creative art assignment. "I want you to draw a picture of someone you really admire," she said. As many good teachers do, she had drawn a picture of someone *she* most admired, so the children could see an example. After most of the children were finished, the teacher found that almost everyone had copied her drawing. One little boy—a CR—was still working on his paper. When the teacher asked who he was drawing, he proudly replied, "This is a picture of God."

The teacher smiled a bit uncertainly and said, "But no one knows what God looks like."

The CR boy just beamed. "They will when I get through!"

The Dominant Concrete Random child is usually full of energy, curiosity, and new ideas. Boredom is the CRs greatest enemy, and school is often viewed as a prison sentence to be served. Formal education must be endured until one can escape into the real world and learn what *really* counts.

Although strong will comes in *all* styles, I have never, in over a decade of teaching learning styles, talked to any dominant CR child or adult who did not admit to being strong-willed. This does not mean CRs are openly rebellious or defiant, only very determined to stay in control of their own lives. CRs do not automatically reject rules and regulations, but they *do* expect to have at least some input into how the rules are made and enforced.

CRs have a nature that resists ultimatums. If you say "do this or *else*," CRs will most likely do "else." They may do it quietly, without fuss, but CRs know there is nothing they really *have* to do except die. Which, by the way, they are willing to do if necessary. Most other styles are not willing to perish over the small things, but CRs are.

When I was younger, my mother and I had a recurring conflict about my messy bedroom. As long as I could find the bed, it was clean enough for me. However, my mother's definition of clean meant I would have to do a lot more than just be able to find the bed. It meant work.

My room was the source of many arguments between us. One day I decided, out of the blue, that I wanted to do something really nice and unexpected for my mother. I determined to clean my bedroom just the way she had always wanted me to do it. Wouldn't that be a wonderful surprise? On the way to my room, my mother intercepted me. It had been a bad day. She was up to her neck in dirty rooms.

Pointing her finger at me, she said, "Cynthia Kay Ulrich, get in your room *right now*. You are not coming out of there until that room is clean."

What I was inspired to do just moments before had suddenly become an ultimatum. I saw it as an edict designed to take all control away from me. I decided there was nothing my mother could do that would compel me to clean my room.

I took the punishment: I got spanked. I got grounded. I went without dinner. Nothing worked. My mother probably could have, at that point, struck a match and set the room on fire and I'd have chosen to perish in the flames.

I had not set out to deliberately disobey my mother. It was only when I felt I had no control that I refused to cooperate. The ultimatum had been issued, and I felt I had no choice but to prove I did not *have* to obey.

The CRs concrete abilities make them masters at separating the letter from the spirit of the law. It is a great resource for accomplishing what the CR wants to do without *technically* having done anything against the rules. "You said don't jump off *this* chair."

Carol, one of the teachers attending one of my classes about teaching strong-willed children, recalled an incident in her childhood that remains a vivid example of her strong-willed, CR nature. She was in elementary school, and the teacher was passing around a pussy willow for the children to look at closely. The teacher told the class that everyone should feel free to touch and play with the pussy willow, but *whatever* they did, they were *not* to put the pussy willow in their ear. Carol was the last one to get the pussy willow. While waiting for her turn to hold it, she almost drove herself crazy wondering *why* the teacher said not to put it in her ear. Why not? What would happen?

When the pussy willow finally got to her, Carol scrunched down in her seat, hid her face, and stuck it not in her ear, but in her nose. It went in easy, but it got stuck coming out, and she ended up having to stand in the corner for quite a while for her little experiment. To this day, she says she feels angry with that teacher. After all, she did *not* put the pussy willow in her *ear*, so she had *not* disobeyed!

Although CR children can easily exasperate their parents, the fact is that CRs expect parents to be in authority. CRs expect boundaries and actually welcome the security of knowing the limits. The greatest challenge comes in how parents communicate that authority, and how much input the CR has into the rules and the consequences.

Several years ago, I was sitting in a family restaurant with my husband when I overheard a heated conversation at the next table. I glanced over and saw a young mom and dad and a small boy about eight years old. The dad slammed his fork down and pointed his finger at his son. "You do this to me every time," he said. "I let you order on your own from the child's menu, and then you don't eat what you order. Well, I'll tell you what, young man, from now on *I'll* do the ordering and *you'll* do the eating."

The boy did not acknowledge that he had heard the new rule at all. His father leaned closer to him. "And we're not leaving here until you've eaten what you ordered today."

I sneaked a look at that young boy's face. Without uttering a word, his expression said, "Bring on the rent receipt book; I guess we live here now." The ultimatum had been given, and the boy obviously had no intention of complying. The father's back was toward me, and I could see the flush begin to creep up his neck. The veins began to bulge, and he was almost shaking with his anger. The mom seemed upset at the turn of events. I could tell she had played this scene many times before. Attempting to smooth the waters, she reached out to her son. "Maybe if you eat something from *my* plate," she began. *"Don't you help him!"* roared the father. *"He's going to do this on my terms!"*

A few minutes later, I watched this family leave the restaurant. The father stormed out, practically on the verge of a cardiac arrest. The mother was in tears, and the child, wearing an indifferent expression, had left behind an uneaten dinner.

I understood the situation better than most. As a mother, I certainly can empathize with those parents. But as a lifelong strong-willed child, I can tell you that in most cases the approach they used does not work.

If I had been that strong-willed child, do you know what would have worked with me? If my dad had said, "Are you going to eat that?" and I had replied, "No," my dad's response would then have been to call the waitress and ask for a doggie bag. He would have turned to me and said, "Fine. You don't have to eat it now, but it *will* be the next thing you eat. You see, the rule is you eat what you order. That's the rule." If my dad let me have some control in deciding under what *terms* I would eat it, he would usually find me complying with the rule. It really is more an issue of control than of authority.

WHAT ABOUT STRESS?

When it comes to recognizing and dealing with stress, the dominant CR parent and child have a lot in common.

The Dominant Concrete Random usually thrives with

inspiration
independence
compelling reasons
freedom to choose options
guidelines instead of rules
opportunities for creative alternatives

The Dominant Concrete Random is often stressed by

excessive restrictions and limitations
forced schedules or routines
not being appreciated as a unique individual
not being given credit for knowing the right thing to do

You can frequently lessen the stress by

lightening up without letting up
backing off, not forcing the issue
helping the CR figure out what will inspire him
encouraging lots of ways to reach the same goal
conveying love and acceptance no matter what

CONCRETE RANDOM

What People with Other Styles Admire Most About the CR

sense of humor

multidimensional personality

creativity

intuition

independence

Negative Perceptions By People with Other Styles

uncompromising

not a team player

too many whys

stubborn

impulsive

Ten Commandments for Getting Along with a CR

Thou Shalt:

keep me involved (we need responsibility and input)

have a sense of humor

tell me "what" not "how"

be open to change

point me in the right direction, then let me go

be flexible

tell me what I did right, not what I did wrong

why do we need ten?

don't be threatened by enthusiasm

know your limits—then push them

Now that you have some understanding of learning styles and have hopefully identified your own, take a piece of paper and draw a picture that illustrates some of the characteristics of your child's or your own learning style. To get you started, here is a picture that represents the characteristics of an Abstract Random learning style. *We are only using the AR style as an example.* If you are a different learning style, your picture will look very different.

Save your picture. We will be adding more learning style elements to it as we go along.

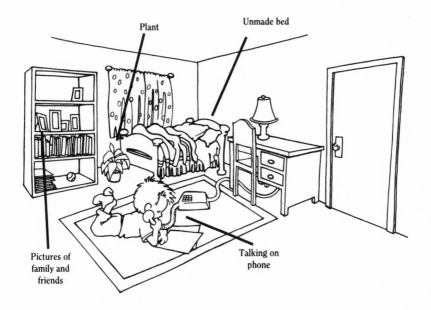

In a Nutshell

I frequently tell parents of strong-willed, CR children that those kids are going to change the world. It's not likely the world is going to change *them*! Once you begin to understand CR strengths, you will be amazed at how much CRs contribute to keeping the world moving and growing and changing. Instead of fighting to force CRs to conform, perhaps we should take a little more notice of how many of their ideas have real merit. The CR in all of us may just save us from ourselves!

Chapter Seven

How Do We Concentrate?

Now that you have a basic grasp of Gregorc's description of how our minds work, let me add another layer to the overall picture. We all have certain preferences for our most productive learning environments. Such things as the way a room is lighted or heated, if the chairs are comfortable or not, if we are hungry or not, can all influence our ability to concentrate.

Identifying these environmental preferences will add an important dimension to our understanding of learning styles.

Several years ago, I tuned into an afternoon talk show touting an educational consultant. He had just written a book designed to help parents get their reluctant children to do homework. The producer had invited several sets of frustrated mothers and their children. The host let the author and the mothers interact with each other candidly.

Although each mother's story was different, the "homework expert" repeated the same solution for everyone: "Make the task of doing homework an absolutely relentless pursuit. Outline to your child what is expected, and don't give up until he or she has made this a habit."

One mother had her 12-year-old son by the shoulders. "But my son gets distracted by *everything*!" she exclaimed. The homework expert shook his head. "Then you aren't making this whole procedure important enough in your family routine," he admonished. The already frustrated mother made an exasperated gesture and guided her son off the stage.

Another harried mother spoke up. "I have tried *everything* to get my daughter to do her homework short of threatening to *kill* her. *Nothing* works." The expert smiled indulgently and insisted, "You just have to make it important enough."

One by one I watched the mothers leave in despair, certain that not only was their child not doing homework, but that it was somehow their *fault* for not being firm enough or dedicated enough to finding a solution.

Getting children to do homework illustrates how difficult it can be for them to concentrate and focus on learning. Although many factors have been blamed for this lack of attention, I believe that perhaps the most logical, reasonable causes have been largely overlooked.

As parents, it is quite natural for us to insist that our children study and approach learning tasks in the ways that make sense to *us*. After all, we are living proof of what does and does not work. Right?

But think about it. How many of you who are reading this book married someone exactly like you? It is rare. (Isn't it interesting how we are drawn to those so different from us for their "refreshing perspective," and then find ourselves so annoyed by the contrasts between our styles on a day-to-day basis?) Now if you and your spouse are so dramatically different in your approaches to life, just think of the myriad of combinations your children will exhibit!

But wait! All is not lost! We can learn to use our children's choices of *environmental preferences* to help them concentrate and learn. Let's look at some different study environments and see which are best when a person really needs to concentrate and learn effectively.

Among the leading researchers in this field is the husband and wife team of Kenneth and Rita Dunn.[1] The Dunns have spent years studying the effects of environment on an individual and the individual's inborn learning style as it relates to concentration and remembering information. (See the bibliography for more on this topic.) Using the Dunn's research, let me highlight a few important factors every parent should consider while trying to find the most effective way to help their children concentrate.

WHERE SHOULD YOUR CHILDREN STUDY?

The traditional idea of giving our children a suitable place to study has been around for generations. The standard approach is to insist upon a consistent time each evening, provide a clean, quiet, well-lit room with a desk and chair, and make sure the room and the child are free of distractions. For many children, as well as adults, this is a very effective way to concentrate. For some of us, however, it is tantamount to being imprisoned without possibility of parole.

I have always favored working on the floor, both as a student and as an adult. Even if I'm dressed in a business suit, I close my office door and spread everything out on the floor before commencing my work. At home, my husband will often find me hunched over books and papers on the floor, lost in thought. He is concerned.

"The light is terrible in here!" he exclaims. "And you're going to ruin your back sitting on the floor like that. Here, here! We have a perfectly clean and wonderful rolltop desk." He sweeps up my papers and neatly places them on the desk, helps me into the chair, turns on the high-intensity lamp, and pats my shoulder.

"Now, isn't that better?" he asks.

I nod and wait until he is down the hall and out of sight. Then, I gather all my papers and go back down on the floor. You see, I could sit at the rolltop desk for as long as he really needed me to sit there. But that's all I'd be doing—sitting at the rolltop desk. I could sit there for an hour, and when he came back, I wouldn't have done anything. "What's the matter?" he'd ask. "You've had ideal conditions: an hour of uninterrupted time and a clean, well-lit place to work. Why haven't you *done* anything?" It does not occur to him that anyone in their right mind could actually work better on the floor than on the desk, or concentrate better in 10-minute spurts with music or noise in the background than in a silent 60-minute block of time.

Sitting on the couch or curling up on the floor is the only way some people can be comfortable enough to really concentrate. Because of our individual preferences, it's important to remember that *our* way won't always work for everybody in our family. Instead of insisting on a particular place for your child to study, try watching what position your child uses most often when engrossed in a book or other favorite task, and let him use the same position for studying.

How Quiet Should It Be?

Some parents have a hard time imagining that a person could actually *need* noise to keep from being distracted. I, for one, am greatly distracted by solitude and silence. My husband, on the other hand, is *dependent* upon those two elements for any constructive task. We have yet to see what kind of study environment our sons will need. Because they are not alike, except in the way they look, they will probably each have a very different environmental work preference.

Often parents will express surprise that their children seem to get the most homework done while sitting in the middle of the living room with the television on and other family members coming and going. Many students tell me they do their best work while lying comfortably on a bed. Others claim they have to be sitting in hard chairs in order to stay alert.

What About Light?

At some point in our lives, most of us have heard our moms tell us, "Turn on the light or you'll ruin your eyes!" The truth is, we all seem to have different levels of tolerance for bright or dim light. In most families, there is at least one person who goes around turning *off* lights behind the person who is turning *on* every light in the house. Although public schools insist upon using bright overhead florescent lights, some students may *lose* concentration because they need a softer light. Experiment with different levels of light in order to find out what is most comfortable and produces the best learning environment for your child. The key is to use enough light to see without having to strain your eyes. Remember, the chances are very good that *your* preferences will be different from those of your children!

Should You Turn up the Heat?

If you walk into almost any classroom around the country, you will usually find some students sitting comfortably in lightweight, short-sleeved shirts while others are shivering in their sweaters or jackets.

When it comes to an ideal room temperature, there are physical differences between individuals. If the temperature is too hot or too cold, many students will be unable to concentrate. While some adapt easily to varying temperatures, others need the room to be comfortable before they can pay attention to anything else.

One of my favorite anecdotes was related during a workshop by Rita Dunn, the researcher I mentioned earlier in this chapter. As she was working with young students who were studying English as a second language, she was trying to test their knowledge of basic words. "What is a 'sweater'?" she asked the children. One small boy near the front immediately raised his hand and answered matter-of-factly: "It's what your mother makes you wear when she's cold."

Should Students Be Allowed to Eat While Studying?

It has been a long-standing rule in traditional classrooms that no food or drink is allowed. For some children, this is not a problem, since eating or drinking might distract them from listening and concentrating. For others, however, eating or drinking may actually be necessary to keep their minds focused on what they are doing. If you need to have a cup of coffee or can of soda handy while working, you probably understand why many students are distracted when they must listen to a teacher or work on an assignment when they are hungry or thirsty.

If you see a student chewing on a pencil or gnawing on the end of a ruler, it could be that he or she is desperately trying not to think about the hunger pangs that are threatening to overshadow any academic thoughts. Although it's not always practical to have food and drink in a classroom, often just a piece of hard candy or chewing gum is enough to help a hungry student concentrate on what's being taught instead of thinking about the lunch break.

LISTENING TO THE INTERNAL TIME CLOCK

Since I have always been a morning person, I was surprised to find out that there are those who are actually *annoyed* by people who appear too alert or cheerful before 10 A.M. On the other hand, I'm ready to call it a day before the 11 o'clock news, while the night people are just getting their greatest spurt of energy. Although we can discipline ourselves to cope at just about any time of day, most of us have certain hours when we are naturally more energetic.

If you have one child who is most alert in the morning and another child who is the proverbial night owl, it's unrealistic to expect them both to do their best job on homework at the same time of day. It also stands to reason that when a student needs to take a difficult or boring class, he will succeed better if that class is scheduled during his most alert time of day. If that is impossible, he may at least be able to do his homework during his peak performance hours. If he can, his concentration will be greatly improved.

Recently, I met with several classes of high school students to discuss study skills. I set up the following scenario:

> Suppose you are wavering between an A and a B for a semester grade in history. The upcoming final exam will determine your semester grade. If you get an A on the final, you will get an A for the semester. If you get anything lower than an A on the final, your semester grade will be a B.
>
> Your parents are quite anxious that you get the highest possible grade for the semester. They're so eager, that they've promised you a car in exchange for your outstanding performance on the final. Take the large sheet of paper and draw a picture of where you will study for this all-important test. Draw in as much detail as possible: location, lighting, refreshments, etc., in your ideal study spot.

When the students finished, they initialed their drawings and posted them. Several students were given the opportunity to explain their ideal study situations. Throughout the sharing, students who were not sharing kept exclaiming, "You study in your bedroom? No way! I'd fall asleep if I tried that!" or "I have to have daylight or I just can't concentrate," or "I could never study *outside!*" When the discussion was over, I asked them an important question:

"So, what *is* the right study situation?" The answer was simple and unanimous. "It's the one that works best for *you*."

A RADICAL EXPERIMENT FOR GETTING YOUR CHILD TO DO HOMEWORK

Many parents say that their children have some pretty ridiculous claims about where and when they *like* to do homework. These parents wonder how anyone can work late at night on the couch with a can of pop and the radio on. If getting your child to do homework is becoming an almost impossible chore, here is an approach that may at first seem a bit radical. But keep an open mind!

Strike a deal with your reluctant student. For two weeks, agree to let the student study at home any *time*, in any *place*, with any *thing* he or she says is needed (within the laws of the land and the rules of the household, of course). If, at the end of that two weeks, he turns in his homework and his grades are improving, you will accept that your child really *does* know how to study best. If, however, homework is still *not* being turned in and grades are *not* improving, the student must agree to abide by *your* study methods.

For best results, contact your child's teacher before the two-week period begins. Discuss what you're proposing, and ask the teacher to help you judge whether or not your child's work improves or goes downhill during the trial period.

I find that although students may begin by trying some pretty outrageous methods during the first two or three days, they also realize they must prove that their ways *work*. In the end, many will actually move closer to the methods their parents had in mind in the first place. Interestingly enough, parents find *they* have been able to effectively compromise in ways that may never have occurred to them.

One frustrated mother claimed her daughter was simply trying to use her learning style as an excuse to watch a favorite television show. "My daughter says she can only do her hardest homework during this half-hour television show." I suggested she call her daughter's bluff. If it was a television show approved by her parents, let her do her homework during the show. At the end of the show, however, collect the homework. After all, the daughter must prove her claim is true. Accountability must stay intact!

A Note: It's important to remember that not all of these categories of environmental preferences are equally important to all people. Certain environmental factors may matter a great deal to some. Other factors may just be a bonus. For example, I concentrate better when I can eat or drink something while I am working, but I *can* work without it. I can't work at *all* if I'm cold. Try to identify the elements that are absolutely essential to your child's ability to concentrate successfully. Then, work at achieving as many environmental preferences as possible, as often as possible.

Remember, too, that children should not be able to use their learning styles as an excuse to avoid doing something that doesn't come naturally or sound fun. If you define the specific outcomes you want your children to accomplish, you can then help them achieve those outcomes in a way that makes the most sense to *their* natural learning styles. The chances for their success will be much greater. In circumstances where you cannot accommodate your children's natural learning styles, you can help them understand and cope with the demands of doing whatever they must by recognizing, and then talking with them, about *why* they may find the task frustrating. You can show them how to identify and use their natural strengths to do those things that don't come easily for them.

PUTTING IT INTO ACTION

The following suggestions can help you identify some of your child's natural environmental preferences. As you work through these suggestions, you may discover some of your *own* learning style strengths. Sharing *your* preferences with your child can help both of you understand and appreciate your similarities and differences.

- Give your child a large piece of paper and some markers or crayons. Ask your child to draw a picture of the ideal study place. Ask for as many specific details as possible, and let your child have the opportunity to explain the drawing to you.
- If your child is finding it difficult to identify his preferences, it may help to set up situations that contrast the differences. For example, have

your child try doing a portion of homework in a brightly-lit room and another portion in an area where the lights are at a lower level. Ask him which lighting made it easier to concentrate. (Be prepared for the answer "It doesn't matter." Remember, sometimes it really doesn't.)

• Challenge your child to design, create, or describe the ideal study spot at home. Then, as much as is possible, try to make it become a reality.

Find the drawing you made when you finished the last chapter. Now add some elements that show your most important environmental preferences. Do you need a lot of light? Do you like the room to be warm?

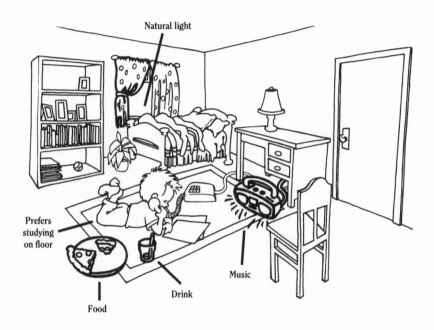

In a Nutshell

Not everyone benefits from the same circumstances and surroundings when it is necessary to concentrate and work. The bottom line is this: Do you know what works for you? Do you know what works for each of your children? Even if you have to change your idea of what "good studying" looks like, you may discover that more homework gets done in an environment that fits individual learning style. You may even find out that some of us *need* chaos to accomplish order!

Chapter Eight

How Do We Remember?

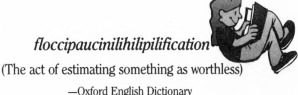

floccipaucinilihilipilification
(The act of estimating something as worthless)
—Oxford English Dictionary

How long would it take you to learn how to spell this word? How would you remember it? Would it be important for you to hear the word pronounced before you learned to spell it?

We use a variety of our five senses when processing and memorizing facts and figures. This is called *sensory perception*. In other words, when we *perceive*, or take in information, we are using one or more of our senses to understand and remember what we perceived.

Here is yet another dimension that can add to our overall understanding of natural learning style strengths and preferences. While Gregorc's model gave us insight into how our minds work and the Dunns' model showed us the diversity of environmental preferences, this model will help us learn several ways of remembering information.

Take this test to determine if you and your children are auditory, visual, or kinesthetic learners.

MODALITY CHECKLIST

Place a check mark by all the statements that strongly describe what you prefer.

Auditory

___I need to hear myself say it in order to remember it.

___I often need to talk through a problem aloud in order to solve it.

___I memorize best by repeating the information aloud or to myself over and over.

___I remember best when the information fits into a rhythmic or musical pattern.

___I would rather listen to a recording of a book than sit and read it.

Visual

___I need to see an illustration of what I'm being taught before I understand it.

___I am drawn to flashy, colorful, visually stimulating objects.

___I almost always prefer books that include pictures or illustrations with the text.

___I look like I'm "daydreaming," when I'm trying to get a mental picture of what's being said.

___I usually remember better when I can actually see the person who's talking.

Kinesthetic

___I have difficulty sitting still for more than a few minutes at a time.

___I usually learn best by physically participating in a task.

___I almost always have some part of my body in motion.

___I prefer to read books or hear stories that are full of action.

Learning styles researchers Walter Barbe and Raymond Swassing[1] present three modes of sensory perception (ways of remembering) that we all use in varying degrees. These are referred to as *modalities*. The most easily recognized modalities are: auditory, visual, and kinesthetic. Let's take a closer look at each of these.

Auditory — Learning by listening to verbal instructions; remembering by forming the sounds of words.

If you are a strong auditory learner, this does *not* necessarily mean you only need to hear something once to remember it. It *does* mean that in most circumstances you need to hear *yourself* say it in order to effectively commit it to memory. If your auditory mode is particularly strong, you may find yourself reading aloud instead of silently, talking to yourself, or repeating instructions to make sure you understand them.

If you have a more auditory child, you may find that putting facts or dates into a song, a rap, or a rhythm of some kind helps them memorize. Listening to how a word *sounds* may be a very important part of learning what the word *means*.

During my years as a police officer, one of my specialties was finding and arresting drunk drivers. A crucial part of determining whether or not a driver was too intoxicated to be behind the wheel was the "field sobriety test." After I put the suspected drunk driver through a variety of balance tests, I always asked the same question at the end. "Could you please say the alphabet for me?"

You see, unless you are a rare case or a hardened alcoholic, you usually can't say the alphabet at a normal conversational rate if you're under the influence of alcohol. If drunk driving weren't so serious, it would have been almost amusing to hear the various versions of the standard alphabet these inebriated individuals recited. Interestingly enough, it seems as though no matter how drunk a person is, he can almost always *sing* the alphabet song. I had more than one person in a business suit standing by the side of the road singing his ABCs just so he could remember how the alphabet started!

It might be wise to insert a word of caution here. Often a strongly auditory parent insists that the not-so-auditory child drills or reviews aloud. If the auditory mode is not particularly strong in the child, he may have to struggle to memorize using this method. In other words, at the end of those precious minutes carved out of a busy evening, you may have a child who knows *less* than when the review began! The frustrated parent believes that the child is simply not paying attention or not trying hard enough to remember. And the child may not even be able to explain *why* he can't remember.

Visual   Learning by seeing and watching; using strong visual associations.

If the *visual* way of learning is particularly strong for you, you may often try to picture in your mind what you are learning. You may even be accused of daydreaming or being lost in thought. The more visual learner usually learns best by associating pictures with the words or concepts being used. When reading or remembering, the visual learner may constantly be imagining what things *look* like and may sometimes be picturing something *very* different than the actual facts!

Because I am a strong visual learner, I began to keep a written record of the names of places that evoked strong mental pictures, even though I realized the images in my mind were probably not entirely accurate. For example, I get a warm, full feeling when I see the street sign in Nampa, Idaho, that tells me I'm walking down *Chicken Dinner Road*. It is not, however, a very positive image that pops into my mind when I read the name of one of the long-standing, used-car lots in Boise: *Fairly Reliable Bob's*. But by far my most vivid visual conjecture is when I drive south of downtown Seattle past a large green building sporting a big sign identifying it as the *Buffalo Sanitary Wipers Company*. Wow! Talk about mental images!

If you have a child who tends to learn more visually, you may find it helpful to encourage the use of brightly colored folders for categorizing papers or eye-catching notebooks for organizing assignments. When reviewing for a test, your visual child may find it most effective to use brightly-colored flashcards. This can help your child concentrate on a visual image for each fact or concept that must be memorized. Even if you're not much of an artist, it often helps the strong visual learner to draw a quick picture that can be associated with what needs to be remembered.

Kinesthetic Learning by becoming physically involved and actually *doing* something with what's being learned.

If you have a child whose *kinesthetic* modality is strongest, you may find him in almost constant motion. All his life he has probably been accused of being "fidgety" or a "wiggle worm." The kinesthetic person hears things like "Sit still!" "Put your feet on the floor!" "No more trips to the drinking fountain!" Although most teachers and parents work hard to get children to be still, the strong kinesthetic child needs to put some sort of action to the learning or the learning doesn't stick! Even if the action is as simple as pacing or moving while reading or memorizing, the more kinesthetic learner will remember best what he learned while on the move.

Anne, a very kinesthetic friend of mine (now a physical education teacher!), admitted that her parents were pretty frustrated with her seemingly endless movements. Her mother would insist Anne stay in her bedroom in the basement until all her homework was done. Finally, this resourceful and restless learner devised a way to learn and still keep moving. She used the basement stairs. For spelling or vocabulary, each stair was a letter or word. For history, each was an important fact or date. For geography, each became a different location. Her mother was puzzled as to why Anne was constantly pounding up and down the stairs. All she knew was that Anne's homework was being done and her grades were improving!

Most strongly kinesthetic children are only able to concentrate on one thing for about 10 minutes at a time without taking some sort of break. Since physical activity is so important, if you are the parent of a kinesthetic child, you may want to suggest he put his homework on a clipboard and do it "on the run." Simply set a specific deadline for the homework to be finished, and let your active child burn up energy while learning! When your child must memorize important information, try associating some sort of bodily movement with what needs to be remembered.

IT REALLY WORKS!

I had been a high school English teacher for three years and was teaching a class called "Intermediate Composition." The class consisted of juniors and seniors who were not motivated enough for advanced composition and not unmotivated enough for the basic class. The administration had all but said that I should not be concerned about making much progress. I was to just do my best to get them through the class so they could graduate. One of my favorite classroom activities was vocabulary exercises. I was determined they would learn to speak and read on a more "educated" level. Each week the students would grudgingly take their vocabulary test, and each week the scores remained very poor.

Toward the end of the semester, I attended a learning conference where the keynote speaker was a learning styles expert. I sat spellbound throughout her presentation. Here was an educator and researcher who suddenly validated what I, as a teacher, had known for a long time: All students *could* learn, but we cannot expect them to learn in the same *way*. This speaker suggested practical methods for different *modality* approaches when trying to teach something that must be memorized.

Back in the classroom on Monday morning, I enthusiastically tried to communicate the information I had learned to my less-than-enthusiastic students. We were getting ready to take the semester test on 84 difficult vocabulary words. Because the weekly tests had resulted in such poor grades, none of the students expected to do much more than barely pass the semester test. I was so sold on this learning styles method that my students became intrigued in spite of themselves. I admitted the whole idea was new to me. I asked them if they would go along with me as an experiment and try studying the vocabulary words for the semester exam in a new way.

I explained to them the three different modalities: auditory, visual, and kinesthetic. I had each student fill out an informal checklist and then speculate on which modality or modalities were strongest for him or her. Then I told them my plan: For the next three days we would devote class time to studying the vocabulary words. To do that we would divide into study groups and each of the groups would use the method that made the most sense for that group's particular modality strength. A student could spend any amount of time in a group and could freely switch to another group.

These were the guidelines for the modality groups:

The *auditory group* drilled each other aloud. Back and forth, one student would say the word, and another would give the definition. There was constant noise in the group, as almost everyone was trying to verbalize the words and their meanings. Fortunately, we had access to an additional room where the auditory group could speak without disturbing the others.

The *visual group* carefully wrote flash cards for each vocabulary word, illustrating each card with an appropriate picture or design. For most of them, the very act of writing and illustrating the cards was enough to help them memorize the words, but they happily used the flash cards to quiz each other.

The *kinesthetic group* was a restless one! Since they preferred to stay in constant motion, I suggested they design body movements for each vocabulary word that would help them remember the definition. They eagerly accepted the challenge and sometimes literally wrestled over how their movements should define the vocabulary words.

The day of the final exam arrived. Normally on the day of a big test, I would hear at least two kinds of pleas from students as they entered: "Oh, please, can we have another day?" or "Quick! Give me the test before it all leaks out!"

That day the students sauntered in confidently, saying, "Bring on the test—I'm ready!" Twenty-nine heads bent to complete the test. I was amused as I watched the kinesthetic group of students take it. They were in constant motion, and at each word, they would pause, their bodies taking on a definite (and often mystifying) pose. Then they would mark an answer and go on.

Out of 29 "mediocre" students, 26 of them did not miss one single item on the test. Among the other three students, no one missed more than five. I had never seen my class so excited! Students who had never gotten an A in their academic life were heady with success. We all discussed why the methods worked and then celebrated with a pizza party.

Feeling somewhat euphoric, I shared my success in the faculty room with several of my fellow teachers. Their responses were like a bucket of cold water being thrown in my face. "The test was probably too easy." "You probably did the studying for them." "They probably cheated." "A fluke—it'll never happen again."

Feeling cheated out of my victory, I mulled over my options. How could I be sure my students really knew the information? Two weeks later, without warning, I gave these same students another test over the same words in a different test format. The grades were almost identical. The students were hurt that I would doubt their knowledge. "Miss Ulrich, we *know* those words!"

Mike was one of my seniors that year, and after graduating, he joined the Navy. For the next two years, each time Mike was home on leave he would show up at the door of my classroom after school. "Hey!" he'd say, "do you still have a copy of that vocabulary test?" I'd pull out the test, and he would quickly mark the answers and proudly present it for scoring. The result? Almost always 82 correct out of 84 (he had trouble with *imminent* vs. *eminent*). He'd grin at me and say, "See? I *told* you I know those words!"

Not all my learning style experiments had such dramatic results, but the learning curve increased *significantly* in most cases. Since my opportunities for varying the style of instruction I used were somewhat limited by administrative policies, I held my own parent/teacher meetings once a month. I helped interested parents develop some support strategies they could use at home for helping their children be more successful in school. Let me share a few of my favorites:

For more auditory learners:

- Offer to drill them verbally, or let them choose a classmate or friend who will drill with them.
- Help them put the information into a rhythmic pattern—perhaps create a poem, a song, or a rap.
- For reading assignments, let them read aloud, maybe even into a tape recorder, and then play it back for review.
- Minimize visual distractions in the study area.

For more visual learners:

- Give them bright colors and large spaces to draw or write.
- Encourage them to take notes or doodle while listening.
- Stress underlining or highlighting information in notes or books when possible so they can draw their own picture (no matter how bad they think it looks) to associate with facts, letters, or words.

For more kinesthetic learners:

- Encourage them to take frequent breaks while studying.
- Offer big spaces to draw and write.
- Provide them with stories to read that are filled with action.
- Instruct them to write notes or highlight information while listening.

There are three ways in which we take in and remember information. They are: auditory, visual, and kinesthetic. Add to your picture elements that illustrate how you take in information. You can be a CS, an AS, an AR, or a CR and can take in information in any of the three ways listed above. Now let's see what the AR in our example does. He is a strongly visual AR learner.

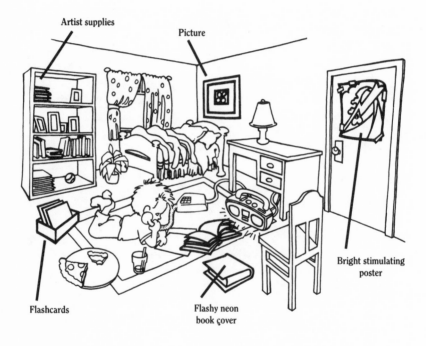

Artist supplies

Picture

Bright stimulating poster

Flashcards

Flashy neon book çover

In a Nutshell

Most people find they are strong in at least two of these modalities, and maybe even all three. No one is restricted to just one modality strength! If you aren't sure whether the auditory, visual, or kinesthetic methods would work best for your child, try out each approach until you find the one that fits. It may even vary from day to day. The important thing is to find the method of remembering and reviewing that works best for each individual!

Chapter Nine

How Do We Understand?

"Can you tell me where to find the library?"

"Sure! Just go down two blocks to the park with the statue in the middle, you know—where they tore the road up last year. Take a right until you get just past the fire station, then go about three more blocks until you see a great big white house with a green picket fence. The library is right across the street."

"I'm sorry, I'm a little confused. Can you tell me street names? Can you give me the address of the library?"

"Huh? Nope. Sorry—I only know how to get there!"

We have already looked at several ways to identify learning styles. The next layer of information can give you a solid grasp on the way you and your children deal with information from the very beginning. As we can see in the story above, when we learn, a fundamental difference occurs in the way each

103

of us takes in and communicates the data. The way in which we take in information affects how we communicate it to others. The Witkin model of learning styles can help us recognize and appreciate this process.

This chapter is dedicated to helping you understand that learners of all ages can benefit by recognizing and using inborn learning strengths for tackling almost any task, assignment, or test. As we focus on the parent/student and teacher/student relationship, you may find unexpected reasons your child is experiencing success or frustration when it comes to learning.

During World War II, the United States Navy made a startling discovery about their fighter pilots. All of these pilots were exceptionally intelligent, incredibly talented, extremely motivated, rigidly screened, and thoroughly trained. However, when flying through a fog bank, some of these pilots would fly out of the mist upside down. This *concerned* the Navy! They could not afford to have pilots in the air who lost their whole sense of being upright when they lost their external field of vision.

The Navy called in a psychological researcher, Herman Witkin,[1] to conduct some tests on the pilots to determine which of them should be flying and which needed more instrument training before they got into any more cloud covers.

Witkin designed a special room for his experiments. He placed each pilot in a chair that tilted inside a room that also tilted. When the pilot was sure he was sitting straight up and down, he was to tell Witkin. Some of these pilots would claim they were sitting straight, and yet when Witkin checked, they and the room were actually tilted—sometimes as much as 30 degrees! They needed the room to be lined up with them in order to feel that they were sitting straight.

It's a lot like the sensation you get at Disneyland's "America the Beautiful" round theater. You're clutching the railing trying to keep from falling off the back of the fire truck you see on the screen. If the lights in the theater came on, you might feel a little silly! Nothing is actually moving. You are standing still and the only thing that's really changed is your external field of vision.

Other pilots tested by Witkin *always* knew when they were sitting straight up, no matter how tilted the room was. Evidently they were not affected as much by their external field of vision as the first set of pilots. This experiment began strictly as a test of physical perception. Almost by accident, Witkin and his associates began to notice some behaviors and traits that were consistent between these two types of pilots when they lost their external field of vision, and the way in which they approached learning tasks.

The pilots who always knew when they were sitting straight regardless of their surroundings tended to be more *field independent,* or *analytic,* when learning new information. They automatically broke down any information given them into component parts and then focused on details. The other pilots, those who needed their external field of vision in order to know when they were sitting straight, tended to approach information in a much more *field dependent,* or *global,* way. That is, they got the overall picture or "gist" of things, but they didn't worry about the details as much. Remember, both types of pilots were intelligent, talented, and motivated. The difference lay not in whether they *could* learn, but how they naturally learned *best.*

Because each person sees the world from his or her own frame of reference (global or analytic), it is possible that even when many people see the same event, they'll have several versions of what actually happened.

As a police officer, I helped investigate many automobile accidents. I would pull up to the scene, locate witnesses, and then begin the challenge of finding out what actually happened. The first witness might give me an accurate description of the cars involved—the year, the make, the model, the color. The next witness wouldn't have a clue about the kind of cars they were, but would launch into a detailed description of each driver. The third witness would look a little embarrassed at not noticing the cars and drivers, but couldn't wait to relate how the accident *happened.*

Did these people see the same accident? Yes, but these varying perspectives reflect the same learning differences the pilots experienced. The people who witnessed the accident were looking at the situation through their own "windows." The analytics were automatically recording details in their minds; the globals were naturally more concerned with the overall picture of what had happened.

As students, the way we approach learning and the effectiveness of our studying and taking tests is also greatly influenced by our natural tendency toward being more *global* or *analytic*. Naturally, no one person is purely one style or the other. But if we can identify some strengths and natural inclinations, we may discover more efficient ways to study and learn.

The following informal survey will help you determine your natural global or analytic strengths. Later you will probably want to give this test to your child or to answer for him if he is too young to take it himself. Answer as honestly as possible, and even though you may want to choose both options on any given statement, always try to choose the one you would do *most* of the time.

What's My Dominant Learning Style?

Place a check mark beside the *one* statement in each pair that best describes your preferences *when you are learning.*

When you are learning, do you *usually:*

    A   **B**

1. __ like learning by yourself better than working with another person or group?
   __ like learning with another person or group better than working by yourself?

2. __ finish one job before going on to the next one?
   __ begin a new job even if you have not finished an earlier one?

3. __ begin your work without waiting to see how someone else does it?
   __ prefer to wait for someone else to start before you begin?

4. __ find it easier to remember details when you read than to remember main ideas?
   __ find it easier to remember main ideas when you read than to remember details?

5. __ prefer true-false and multiple choice tests with one right answer?
   __ prefer tests that ask you to explain reasons and write out answers?

6. __ need to have your desk and work area neat to concentrate?
   __ find you can get your work done even if your desk or work area is cluttered?

7. __ feel your time was wasted if the teacher doesn't put a grade on work you turned in?
   __ not mind the teacher not giving you a grade as long as your work was recognized?

8. __ prefer competing on your own to competing on a team?
   __ prefer competing on a team to competing on your own?

9. __ prefer to have choices as to how to accomplish assignments you're given?
   __ prefer that the teacher tells you exactly how the assignment should be done?

10. __ want to go over a test that's been graded in order to correct what you missed?
    __ want to look over your graded test but do not want to correct specific answers?

11. __ find it fairly easy to ignore distractions while you work or study?
    __ find it pretty difficult to ignore distractions while you work or study?

12. __ prefer to have an assignment in smaller parts and given step-by-step?
    __ need to know the whole assignment before you work on parts or steps?

13. __ prefer to think about a decision and figure out what to do by yourself?
    __ ask other people's opinions if you aren't sure about making a decision?

14. __ not take it personally if someone tells you you've done something wrong?
    __ automatically take it personally if someone says you've done something wrong?

15. __ blame the test if you don't do well and you studied what the teacher told you?
    __ blame yourself if you don't do well on a test and you studied what the teacher said?

__ __ **Column Totals**

Total the number of "check marks" in each column. If the number is greater in column A, you tend to be more *analytic*. If the number is greater in column B, you tend to be more *global*.

Although you got a higher number in one column, remember that there is no *pure* style. All of us are a mixture of *many* style characteristics. The terms *global* and *analytic* are extremes, and most of us will find ourselves to some extent in both categories. Remember, too, that how you came out on the Gregorc model will influence the type of global or analytic learner you are. For example, there's a big difference between an analytic who is Abstract Random and an analytic who is Concrete Sequential!

My husband, John, is extremely analytic by nature. When we watch a movie together, he must watch *every single* credit go by. He reads each name and notes each line of information. If you ask John later what the movie was about, he provides a *lengthy* retelling of the story, complete with snippets of dialogue. I watched the same movie. But because I am a more global learner, if you were to ask *me* what the movie was about, I would probably give you a very general and vague description of the plot. Who starred in the movie? I don't know—some tall guy with brown hair who plays on a TV show. Where was the movie filmed? I don't know—big city, tall buildings, snow on the ground. After all, you didn't tell me there was going to be a *quiz* at the end! You see, I just *experience*d the movie. I don't pay attention to specific details unless you tell me ahead of time what I'm supposed to be looking for.

The global learner sees the *big picture* or overall view, while the analytic focuses on the *parts* that make up the big picture. A more analytic learner figures you have to clearly understand the parts to eventually understand the whole. The more global learner claims there's no point in clarifying a detail if you can't see where it fits into the whole picture. The global sees all the parts as being related to each other and may have trouble breaking down the big picture into separate pieces.

It's a lot like putting together a jigsaw puzzle. As a global, I must constantly see the completed picture on the puzzle box to put the individual pieces together. My analytic husband often prefers to analyze how the shapes of the puzzle pieces fit together. He may put several sections of the puzzle together before he ever concerns himself with how everything fits into the completed picture.

Consider the following lists of characteristics for the analytic and the global learning styles. You'll probably identify with several items from *both* lists, but you may also discover a distinct pattern of preferences when it comes to how you approach and process what you need to know. Remember, this has to do *only* with how you interact with *information,* not necessarily how your global or analytic tendencies may show up in interpersonal relationships.

HOW ANALYTIC ARE YOU?

Analytic Strengths

- details
- focus
- organization
- remembering specifics
- direct answers
- consistency
- sense of justice
- objectivity
- individual competition
- doing one thing at a time

What You Should Know About the Analytic Style

- likes things ordered in a step-by-step way
- pays close attention to details
- must be prepared
- needs to know what to expect
- often values facts over feelings
- prefers to finish one thing at a time
- rarely becomes personally or emotionally involved
- logical
- self-motivated
- finds the facts but sometimes misses the main idea

Analytic Frustrations

- having opinion expressed as fact
- not understanding the purpose for doing something
- not understanding how a teacher grades
- listening to an overview without knowing the steps involved
- listening to an explanation when all that's needed is a "yes" or "no" answer
- dealing with generalities
- having to find personal meaning in all that they learn
- not finishing one task before going on to the next

HOW GLOBAL ARE YOU?

Global Strengths

- seeing the big picture
- seeing relationships
- cooperating in group efforts
- reading between the lines
- sense of fairness
- seeing many options
- paraphrasing
- doing several things at once
- giving and receiving praise
- reading body language
- getting others involved

What You Should Know About the Global Style

- sensitive to other people's feelings
- flexible
- goes with the flow
- learns by discussion and working with others
- needs reassurance and reinforcement
- works hard to please others
- takes all criticism personally
- avoids individual competition

- tries to avoid conflict
- may skip steps and details

Global Frustrations

- having to explain themselves analytically
- not getting a chance to explain themselves at all
- not knowing the meaning for doing something
- having to go step-by-step without knowing where they'll end up
- not being able to relate what they are learning to their own life
- not receiving enough credit for their effort
- having to show the steps they used to get an answer
- accepting criticism without taking it personally
- people who are insensitive to other people's feelings

Whether we are more global or analytic, we tend to assume that others want us to give them information in the same manner we ourselves would want to receive it.

In our home, John is by far more analytic than I, and I am frequently guilty of ignoring his need for specific information in favor of my more general outlook. A classic example is when he asked me where to find a particular item. "It's in the other room," I told him.

He just looked at me and blinked. "What other room?" he asked.

"The dining room."

"*Where* in the dining room?"

"The rolltop desk."

"*In* the rolltop desk or *on* it?"

"In it, I think."

"Toward the front or toward the back?"

"Toward the back."

"On the left or on the right?"

"On the left."

That incident happened a long time ago, and I've learned more about how an analytic mind expects to receive information. Now when John asks me where something is, I pause for a moment. Then I say something like, "It's in the kitchen in the cupboard to the left of the stove on the middle shelf toward the back on the right." He looks at me with a grateful smile and says, "*Thank you* for being so specific!"

Now I may not actually know where the item is, but I know it's close to the place I said. I have discovered that if I start out with very specific information, John doesn't mind continuing the search!

Since the Witkin model deals specifically with how we understand information, let's take a look at the differences between global and analytic learners when it comes to study skills.

PAYING ATTENTION

Your naturally dominant learning style affects how you listen, what you pay attention to, and what you remember.

When more global learners first hear new information, they take it in by listening for the "gist" of what's being said. They can quickly get the main idea or topic and may even find themselves getting ahead of the speaker. Because it is not natural for them to listen for specific *details*, it may sometimes appear that they haven't been paying attention at all. But they have been getting general impressions and an overall idea of what is being said. Unless more global learners consciously train themselves to listen for details, they may miss significant parts of assignments or lectures.

One mother asked her very global young daughter, "What did you do in school today?"

The daughter replied enthusiastically, "Oh, Mom, it was fun! We studied fractions. And the teacher drew a pizza, then it was a Mercedes sign, and then we all *ate* the pizza!"

Mom asked pleasantly, "Do you have any homework?"

Her daughter looked surprised. "Homework? I don't think so. I didn't hear the teacher say anything about homework."

This global child was so busy *experiencing* the class that little or no thought was given to a specific or bothersome detail like homework.

Let's look at the more analytic learner. When analytics first hear new information, they are usually listening for specific details. Later they may even be able to remember the exact words the speaker said. Since analytics naturally tune in to details, it's sometimes difficult for them to identify the overall *concept* the details are describing. For example, an analytic learner may be able to relate all the facts of a story just read but may not be able to explain the *theme*. The analytic must consciously stretch himself to see and understand the bigger picture.

FOLLOWING DIRECTIONS

The differences between the dominantly global and the dominantly analytic style are especially noticeable when it comes to listening and following directions. For example, when a parent or teacher gives directions, the analytic learner listens carefully, then wants to begin without further interruptions. The global learner may also listen to the directions, but he may frequently ask that the directions be repeated. The global was listening for *what* is supposed to be done, not necessarily *how to do it*. In addition, he is often distracted by wondering what *wasn't* said.

In a recent teaching strategies class, I divided the teachers into two groups—globals and analytics. Both groups were to design a lesson plan that would effectively teach extremely global students about Einstein's Special Theory of Relativity. Since some of the *teachers* were fuzzy about the theory, a physics teacher gave a quick 10-minute overview of it.

After the analytics had shared their detailed and comprehensive lesson plans, the globals got up to share theirs. They seemed a bit sheepish. The spokesperson said, "We have to admit we didn't really hear the explanation of the theory. While the physics teacher was explaining it, we kept thinking things like: *How did Einstein think of this? Where was his laboratory—in his garage? Was Einstein married? How did he find something that would go so fast?* By the time we had worked through those questions in our minds and had tuned in to what the speaker was saying, he was finished talking. We all had the sinking feeling that we were going to look dumb . . . again."

Analytic learners who are listening for details may become particularly frustrated if instructions are repeated. They are already focused on the task and do not want to have to again listen to something they already know. On the other hand, if globals are told there will be no repetition of the instructions and they have to get it the first time, they become particularly stressed because they know they probably won't be able to listen for everything at once.

How do you as a parent or teacher meet the needs of both analytic and global learners? Although there are no simple answers, if you make the general purpose clear before giving the *specifics*, you can often give directions without repetition. First tell us what we're going to do, then tell us how we're going to do it. For example, you may say something like, "We are going to study three major causes of the Civil War. You will need to identify two specific examples for each cause we discuss. Now, let me tell you where you can find these examples."

In some cases, if the process or concept being taught is complex, you simply have to encourage the analytics to have more tolerance for the globals. After all, if the globals didn't understand it the first time and the teacher doesn't repeat it, chances are it will be the analytic students next to these globals who will have to clarify what was said!

ORGANIZATION AND TIME MANAGEMENT

If you were speculating about the kind of learning style a person who teaches time management classes might be, which do you think it would be? You're right! Analytics! And who do you suppose *takes* these time management classes? Right again! Globals! Although both styles can be successfully organized, they usually have very different views of how organization and time management look. Is it any wonder that the standard methods employed in classrooms and at work so often don't work?

An extremely *analytic* English teacher insisted her high school students keep their papers in a three-ring binder under specific categories. Although most students complied, one boy, a true *global*, refused to bring a notebook with him every day. He always wore a military fatigue jacket with multiple pockets and was prepared with pens and paper. Finally, out of frustration with noncompliance, the teacher decided to do something about it.

One day, she stopped her students on the way out of class and told them they must all leave their notebooks on their desks. She would look at them that night and grade them according to whether all the papers were there and filed in the proper categories.

As each student placed a notebook on the desk, this particular boy shrugged off his coat, hung it on the back of his chair, and left. With a sinking feeling, the teacher checked the coat. Sure enough, each pocket was a category, and there wasn't a single paper missing!

It often makes the most sense to analytics to have a place for everything and everything in its place. Globals usually consider themselves organized if they are able to *find* something when they need it, even if they have to rummage through a whole pile of stuff to get it. Even though globals may not *appear* to be organized, you may be surprised at how quickly they can locate what they need.

Because the traditional school system is very analytically structured, the analytic learner's approach to managing time and materials fits and is greatly valued. The more global learners may struggle with organizing notebooks and materials enough to meet the grading requirements of a more analytic teacher. A global learning style often does not fit the traditional analytic school structure.

If you are the parent of a global child who seems to be constantly disorganized, try to help him understand the *need* to be organized. If the purpose of being organized is to be able to locate papers and materials later, your child needs to make sure his system (even if it looks pretty messy and disorganized to you) helps him do that. A good test is whether he can find any paper he needs in 60 seconds or less. If he can, obviously his system works, no matter how it looks. If he can't, his system needs to be improved.

When it comes to improving areas of time management and organization, globals and analytics struggle with different kinds of problems. On the following pages, you will find some of the most consistent areas of frustration for both styles and practical ways for dealing with those frustrations.

THE DOMINANT ANALYTIC

It's hard to work with interruptions. Because the natural bent of the dominant analytic mind is to learn by thinking about one thing at a time, it is very disruptive to his concentration to be focused on a concept or an idea, and then suddenly to have to think about something else. Consequently, the analytic is often much better off studying or working alone, then joining others for a social time *after* his work is done. If you, as a parent or teacher, think of something for the analytic to do or something you need to tell him before he finishes his current task, don't break his concentration by interrupting. Write it down and talk with him when he's finished.

There are too many places to organize at once. The dominant analytic is almost always more efficient when tasks or assignments can be divided into categories or pieces. For him, there is a much greater sense of accomplishment when he can make a big difference in a small place than when he is just barely making a small difference in a big place.

Just before our wedding several years ago, my global nature was running wild with random thoughts and last-minute tasks. I kept mentioning things to John, my analytic bridegroom. I'd say, "Don't forget you promised to mow the lawn before your mother arrives," and "Did you call that man about the contract negotiation?" and "Will you pick up the rings while you're in North Seattle?" Finally, John said, "Cindy, just make me a list." Well, I sat down and wrote out a beautiful "to do" list. I printed every item neatly, numbered each one, and put a space in front of each number so he could check it off after he had accomplished the task. I proudly presented my list, and John politely thanked me. A few minutes later as I walked through the dining room, I saw John sitting at the table recopying my list! "What's wrong with my list?" I asked.

He held up the piece of paper he was using to recopy the original list. The paper was neatly divided into four categories: "Personal," "Wedding," "Business," and "Miscellaneous." "You have everything clumped together on the same list," he replied a little incredulously. "You shouldn't have put contract negotiation (a necessary business task) and mowing the lawn (a nice thing to get done if there's time) on the same nonspecific list!" Once he had sorted my list, he began to work in earnest on accomplishing the tasks.

There needs to be some sort of system. The dominant analytic works best when there is a definite and consistent method of doing things, especially if he can create the system himself. Keeping a daily schedule and/or lists of things to do often helps the analytic keep a sense of structure and predictability. Analytics are usually most comfortable when they can set and meet specific goals, preferably on a daily basis.

THE DOMINANT GLOBAL

It's easier to get an organizational system than to keep it. Dominant globals often have what could be called a "pile and bulldoze" system of organizing papers and materials. They start out with all the best intentions of filing things away, but after they find and use something, they frequently toss it into a to-be-filed box, intending to put it where it belongs later. Before they know it, there is a huge pile of papers that practically needs to be bulldozed. A helpful tip is to simplify the system as much as possible so it will be easy for them to put things back. Big baskets or colorful files that hold very general categories of things will encourage at least getting papers back in the right area.

Once in awhile, even globals can become overwhelmed with lack of order. When I finally get to the point of actually cleaning and organizing my office, the first thing I do is take a trip to the store. I have a wonderful time shopping among the colored baskets, plastic drawers, and portable filing systems. When I get back to the office with my bounty, I'm usually out of the mood to organize, and I happily go back to work—in the chaos.

It's too easy to become distracted. The dominantly global mind seems to be going in many directions almost all the time. Just as the global is focused on one task, something else comes up that also has to be taken care of, and instead of finishing the first task, the global begins on the new one and works until something *else* distracts him from the previous task. One of the best ways to overcome this tendency to become distracted is to work with another person. You can promise to help each other finish one thing before going on to another. It's surprising how much easier it is to concentrate when someone else is working with you!

"I'll do it" doesn't always mean "I'll do it now." Often dominantly global students have the very best of intentions, but don't always follow through quickly enough for parents or teachers who have asked them to accomplish

a task. Procrastination is a real temptation for globals, and it can cause a lot of conflict with the analytics in their lives. If you want the global to do something *now*, try offering to work with him at least to get him started. For example, as a global, I often just need a "jump-start." If you will work alongside me even for a few minutes, the chances are very good that I will go ahead and complete the task.

GETTING THE BEST OF THE TEST

Although neither learning style necessarily *likes* tests, dominantly analytic students don't seem to feel as threatened or nervous about them as the more global students are. Dominantly global students usually take tests much more personally than their analytic classmates. Globals often believe that the teacher is out to trick them or make them feel dumb. To them the whole testing situation feels stiff and formal, and sometimes they do poorly on a test because they literally "psyche" themselves into failing.

Dominant analytic students, on the other hand, seem to approach tests with more confidence. Because the analytic nature automatically breaks down information into component parts, the analytic student has an easier time dividing a test into manageable pieces. If the analytic dreads a test, it's usually because he is not prepared and not because he feels the teacher is out to get him.

One of the biggest frustrations for globals is that they understand the whole concept but struggle with the specific and objective testing techniques that seem to suit analytics perfectly. If globals can gain more confidence in nitty-gritty test-taking skills, they will find they are much smarter than their test scores show.

Both my sister Sandee and I are global. We were talking to a physics teacher when Sandee brought up an interesting question. "If a microwave oven can make things *hot* fast, why can't they invent something that would make things *cold* fast?" The teacher smiled indulgently and stated that it was against the laws of physics. He then patiently defined and explained the law. When he finished, Sandee echoed the question on my mind. "OK, but if a microwave oven can make things *hot* fast . . ." His definition had just sped over the top of our heads!

My husband, who is a great interpreter in such matters, stepped in. "It's like this," he explained. "Suppose you had 1,000 ping-pong balls in a net, and the net was tied to the ceiling. If you released the net, the ping-pong balls would quickly spread all over the room. That's the concept behind the microwave. In order to *reverse* the process, you'd have to gather up all the ping-pong balls, put them back in the net, and reattach it to the ceiling."

Got it. I still couldn't tell you what the law is called or take a test on it to save my life, but I understand the concept of how it works. Unfortunately for us globals, we rarely get credit in school for understanding a global concept if we can't pass a test on the analytic details.

I recently asked several groups of teenage students to give me some test-taking tips. Although the analytic groups began serious consideration right away, the globals first listed items like "Lose a contact so you can't take the test," "Stage a fire drill," and "Get a paper cut and bleed on the test so your teacher will feel sorry for you."

After some discussion, the analytic and global students who have successfully coped with all sorts of tests shared some of their secrets. It won't be hard to see the difference between these two lists!

Test Tips from Dominant Analytic Students

- Scan the test quickly to see how many essay, multiple choice, and true-false questions you'll have to answer. Then divide your time according to how long you have to take the test.
- Do the easy questions first; skip the ones that look hard or complex and come back to them later.
- Keep your desk or work area completely clear of clutter; it will help you concentrate during the test.
- Always have an extra pen or pencil during the test.

Test Tips from Dominant Global Students

- Dress comfortably the day of the test.
- Eat something before the test so you won't feel hungry.
- After you have studied for the test, get together with a small group of classmates and review by testing each other.

- Don't come to class too early the day of a test or you may get confused by all the last-minute cramming.

During a short presentation at a youth conference, I noticed a seventh-grade girl listening intently and enthusiastically to everything I said about learning styles and study skills. When the session was over, she bolted out the door and I heard her yell to her friend, "Hey, Stacy! I'm not dumb—I'm *global!*"

FIGURING OUT TEACHERS

No teacher is going to be *just* global or *just* analytic. But it is often helpful for students to look at certain teacher behaviors and preferences. It may help them understand why they are experiencing frustration in those teachers' classrooms.

Parents and students might think it would be best for the teacher and student to have the same dominant learning style. However, this is not necessarily the case. Sometimes, the best situation is for a more global student to be in an analytic teacher's classroom. The analytic teacher can give the global student much-needed structure; and sometimes an analytic student does best in a global teacher's classroom because, there, he can get the big picture rather than just focusing on details.

Since most teachers will be a *mix* of global and analytic behaviors and preferences, it is important to recognize which learning style demands the teacher is making of his students. Understanding what the teacher expects from students is more important than trying to figure out the teacher's dominant style. To help you identify which learning style your child's teacher demands, here are five basic areas where the global or analytic expectations are evident.

Classroom Environment

You can often determine whether a teacher is more global or more analytic just by looking at his classroom. A global teacher may have a classroom that is designed to look like a home away from home. There are posters, plants, rugs, and couches. To the analytic that may look like a whole lot of junk. But to the global, it's "atmosphere."

An analytic teacher's room may look pretty bare by contrast. When you walk into the analytic teacher's classroom, you may find fire drill instructions, daily announcements, and charts and graphs relevant to the day's lesson. Anything else would be considered a distraction. Analytic teachers often keep their classrooms as clean and organized as possible so that the student can concentrate on learning and not the environment.

During a summer class for teachers, one analytic teacher admitted that she was completely prepared for the next fall. She had, in fact, layered her bulletin board so that each month would already be posted. She was soundly "booed" by the globals!

Classroom Organization

Teachers with a strong analytic style will almost always have a set of classroom rules printed and distributed to students at the beginning of the year. The rules, as well as the consequences, are stated specifically so there won't be any confusion.

More global teachers will simply have one or two general classroom rules. For example, "Be kind and courteous to everyone" or "Respect others." Then, when other situations come up requiring the application of specific rules, a global teacher simply handles the problems on a case-by-case basis.

Attitude Toward Students

Global teachers place a high priority on self-esteem and will even teach lessons on self-esteem before they teach their subject matter. The global teacher is convinced that students cannot be successful unless they first have confidence in themselves.

Now, analytic teachers *also* believe that self-esteem is important, but they believe that you achieve self-esteem by experiencing success. So dominantly analytic teachers may set high standards and may seem to be hard on their students because they want the student to succeed in order to gain self-esteem.

Sometimes it's hard for global students to feel that an analytic teacher cares very much about them. In reality both analytic and global teachers can have equal amounts of compassion, but it is just expressed in different ways.

Suppose an important faculty meeting is scheduled at 3:00 P.M. At 2:55, an analytic teacher is rounding the corner, headed for the door of the meeting room. A distraught student intercepts him and asks for help. Chances are good that the analytic teacher will pause, calm the student as much as possible, then set a time to meet with the student later, either after the meeting or before school the next morning.

Now, let's say that the same distraught student intercepts a *global* teacher five minutes before the meeting starts. Chances are better than not that the global teacher will never make it to the meeting. Does either teacher care more? No. Both teachers have compassion but each expresses it in a different way.

Teaching the Content

When it comes to teaching the content of a lesson, more analytic teachers use a lot of lectures, individual activities, and reading projects. They encourage students to work independently and may sometimes appear almost unfriendly to global students.

A more global teacher tends to use discussion, group activities, and cooperative learning. Since global teachers seek to make the subject matter personally important to every student, they often share personal experiences and expect their students to do the same. This can make an analytic very uncomfortable or impatient.

Grading Practices

Analytic teachers almost always have a set grading scale. If 92-100 points is an A and a student gets 91.8 points, an analytic teacher will give the student a B. Dominant analytic teachers often have very specific grading criteria, and the student can count on that teacher to be consistent. Analytic teachers may appear not to give out many compliments, but when that teacher says "good," it may very well be the highest praise you'll receive from him or her!

Global teachers don't like to be very specific with grades. If 92 is an A and a student gets 91.8, the global teacher may say, "Close enough," depending on how hard the teacher believes the student worked. Dominantly global teachers emphasize class participation and may even grade on how often contributions are made to class discussions or group work. Global teachers will usually give their students a lot of positive feedback, complimenting them on things that may not have anything to do with their classroom work.

Parents and students need to understand that *every* style of teacher can contribute a great deal to a student's success. The key to achieving success is how well students understand what the teacher is doing or is asking them to do.

We cannot put people in boxes and say everyone is just like everyone else who has the same learning style. We do people a terrible injustice when we categorize them. A CS, an AS, an AR, or a CR may have all of the characteristics we attribute to those categories and yet may be very global, or at the other extreme, very analytic.

This can be confusing and may not seem to fit. We may not think a CS with a global way of thinking is a possibility. But it happens. It is also possible for an AR to have a strong analytic side.

Because you are not just a "pure" learning style, add to your picture what you might find in the room that would indicate you are a global or an analytic. Look at our example of a global AR to get some ideas.

In a Nutshell

Understanding information is fundamental to almost everything we do on a day-to-day basis. Knowing if we naturally understand information analytically or globally can help us step outside our dominant style and use a completely different style. Understanding that we can make this switch is especially valuable in an academic setting. It is equally important in the areas of business and communication in general. If I don't understand what you mean, how can I know what you're saying?

Chapter Ten

How Many Ways Can We Be Smart?

Do you feel smart?

How do you even know whether or not you *are* smart?

Who *decides*, anyway?

For generations, parents have been led to believe they should use IQ tests to determine where to place their children in school or what kind of programs might be most appropriate. If you've been reading this book in sequence, you've probably already discovered that intelligence comes in *all* styles. It doesn't even *look* the same in all styles. We've been trained as parents and teachers to value the limited kind of intelligence that conforms to a traditional school system's style of learning: logic and mathematical skills, verbal and written communication skills, and analytical and organizational abilities. If you or your child happens to be smart in a way that isn't measured or valued in school, you get the idea that others are smarter and more successful than you are. *But that just isn't true!*

Several years ago, Howard Gardner, a Harvard professor and eminent researcher, released compelling evidence that each human being possesses *many* intelligences. Each of those intelligences appears to be housed in a different part of the brain. So far, Dr. Gardner has been able to identify seven, and he's still working on discovering others.

Educators, realizing the importance of this research, are beginning to adopt a multifaceted model for schools that incorporates the multiple intelligences. When it is adopted, Dr. Gardner's model will make a profound difference in the restructuring of public schools in America. Instead of rote drill and repetition of facts, the multiple intelligence approach helps children experience learning by gaining hands-on experience through apprenticeships. Instead of simply memorizing facts about civil wars and conflicts, students gain an understanding of why wars happen in the first place and what can be done to prevent them. Without compromising academic outcomes, the multiple intelligence model can help students succeed in learning by identifying and using their natural intelligence strengths to cope with almost any task.

This chapter contains a brief overview of this important research. For a more thorough grasp, read Howard Gardner's book *Frames of Mind* and Thomas Armstrong's book *7 Kinds of Smart* (see bibliography).

Unlike other learning style traits we have discussed, Gardner's research claims that intelligence is not fixed at birth, nor does it remain consistent throughout a lifetime. It grows, changes, and develops with the passing of time and with the opportunities afforded the individual. Parents and educators need to recognize and appreciate as many different areas of intelligence as possible within each child. Standard IQ tests may measure how well a person is likely to perform in the current, traditional school system, but the tests do not even come close to predicting a child's potential for success in life after he leaves school.

The principal of a private school recently admitted to me that the administration loves the traditional, sequential, well-behaved students. "But," she confided, "we're very *nice* to those students who struggle with school, because they are often the ones who end up making lots of money and later come back to endow the school!"

According to Gardner's findings, everyone can develop a reasonable use of all seven intelligences, although the chances are good that each person tends to shine in two or three and must struggle to become more adept in the others. As you look through the brief descriptions, you will probably have no trouble identifying those that come easily for you. Regardless of what you may have been taught, any or *all* of these intelligences indicate that you are smart. And remember, no one has to be good at *everything*!

Linguistic

Linguistic intelligence has to do with verbal abilities, and those who possess great amounts of this kind of intelligence tend to be very good at writing, reading, speaking, and debating. Many journalists, teachers, and poets find themselves gifted with a high degree of linguistic intelligence. Because conventional IQ tests place a great deal of value on linguistic abilities, a person who is linguistically inclined usually is considered to be very smart. The more linguistic person often has and uses an extensive vocabulary and tends to be particularly skilled with word games and semantics.

My husband John is highly linguistic. He uses language very literally and chooses his words carefully when speaking. Early in our dating relationship, we had an argument. I am not very good at apologizing, but in one of my rarer moments, I swallowed my pride and gulped out the words "I'm sorry." He calmly turned to me and said, "*Sorry* is a statement of condition; *apologize* is the active verb. Now are you sorry, or do you apologize?" Although *no* more words were exchanged *that* evening, I had come to realize the importance he placed on phrasing!

Just because you may not be gifted linguistically doesn't mean you can't develop enough linguistic skills to survive and conquer the challenges of a society who values them. In Armstrong's book *7 Kinds of Smart*, you will find a list of ways you can deliberately develop linguistic as well as the other intelligences.

Logical-Mathematical

Logical-mathematical intelligence has to do with an individual's abilities in numbers, patterns, and logical reasoning. Although I have to admit the very *thought* of this intelligence makes me break out in a cold sweat, I do believe everyone needs to possess at least a basic understanding of the tenets of math and logic. Certainly if the logical-mathematical comes easily for you, you should score high on traditional IQ tests. Those who are naturally gifted in logical-mathematical intelligence are often the greatest scientists, mathematicians, and philosophers. On a more practical basis, you need logical-mathematical intelligence to successfully cope with balancing a checkbook or grasping the significance of the national debt.

My more logical and sequential friends are usually horrified to find I don't balance my checkbook. I *do* call the toll-free number periodically to make sure I'm in the ballpark, and I never have bounced a check, but I have real difficulty with the detailed reconciliation on my bank statement. On the other hand, my mother-in-law balances her bank statement *immediately* upon receipt. For me it's more practical to simply switch banks every couple years and get a fresh start!

It is important to recognize that logical-mathematical intelligence doesn't mean you have to be a math whiz. So much of our lives are involved with the mysteries of the scientific universe that most of us don't even realize how much logical-mathematical intelligence we already use. Maybe if we can stop thinking about numbers and logic in cold impersonal terms, we can make them more appealing for everyone.

Spatial

Spatial intelligence gives you the ability to think in vivid mental pictures, re-creating or restructuring a given image or situation. Those who are gifted spatially can often look at something and instantly pinpoint areas that could be changed to improve or alter its appearance. Highly spatial professions include architecture, drafting, and mechanical drawing. In almost any given situation, those with spatial intelligence have the natural ability to see what something *could* be as easily as what it is.

My statistics professor in college, a man highly gifted spatially, insists that he is a basically an *intuitive* person. "For example," he said, "when I drive to a place I've never been before, I look at a map and memorize it visually. As I head to my destination, I mentally bring up the map and 'intuitively' drive right to it."

For those of us who are not as gifted spatially, it is easy to recognize that this professor's skill in locating his destination has little to do with intuition. It is his acute spatial ability that allows him to visually re-create an accurate map in his mind's eye.

You might recognize a spatial exercise on a standard IQ test as one of those cubes flattened out, with your task being to state which side will be on top when the cube is reconstructed. Does this look familiar?

These squares will fold into a box which is open at the top. Which letter would mark the BOTTOM of the box?

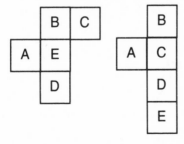

Don't let it make you feel less smart if you can't automatically see the relationships!

Musical

Musical intelligence expresses itself through a natural rhythm and melody, and one who is gifted in this area often seems to live as if life is set to music. Although you may not have "an ear for music" or "perfect pitch," you can still possess a great deal of inherent musical appreciation ability. Many people need music in the background when they are working, and they find themselves tapping their feet almost subconsciously. If you are high in musical intelligence, you may listen to music more analytically than most, appreciating the nuances others may miss altogether.

Cathy, a young mother, told me that she felt at a distinct disadvantage with her 10-year-old daughter, Michelle. "Although we're both musically inclined," Cathy said, "Michelle tends to be too analytic for me to really enjoy listening to a performance with her. As we're listening to a classical piece, she'll pause and say, 'There—listen. Do you hear that French horn?' As I'm struggling to pick it out, she's already identifying a 'really cool bass guitar bridge.' And I thought it just sounded like a nice song!"

Many children are drawn to music and are eager to try their hand at a musical instrument at home or school. Unfortunately when a school district must make budget cuts, one of the first programs to go is the music program. There are many ways we can incorporate musical abilities into our homes and classrooms, and if we can become more effective in our efforts to build on our children's musical strengths, we may find ourselves singing their praises!

Bodily-Kinesthetic

Bodily-kinesthetic intelligence reflects a high degree of ability in bodily movement or physical activity. This includes those who can skillfully use their hands, such as surgeons or mechanics; those who so beautifully bring art to life, such as actors, actresses, and artists; and those who vigorously pursue a blend of physical activity and mental strategies, such as athletes and coaches. Although schools are highly enthusiastic about physical education and sports activities, the bodily-kinesthetic intelligence is not often valued as a way of being smart. In fact, sometimes a gifted athlete who can't be as successful linguistically as another student is accused of being a "dumb jock." It's time we recognize and value kinesthetic intelligence instead of considering only quiet academic intelligence an indicator of accomplishment.

Two adult sisters came to me after a seminar I had given on the subject of multiple intelligences. They had tears in their eyes as they related the story of their dad, who had dropped out of school in the eighth grade and had gone on to earn a living as a woodworker. His cabinetry and furniture was absolutely flawless and in great demand. Even though his workmanship shows great kinesthetic intelligence, he has always felt inadequate. His self-esteem has suffered for years, because he is convinced that it is not possible to be smart if you didn't successfully complete school.

The bodily-kinesthetic person can often "feel things in their bones," and their lives are full of physical activity. The more we try to force these folks to sit still, the more restless their minds become and the less effective formal instruction can be. Instead of fighting their need to move, we need to find ways to channel this energy into positive learning.

Interpersonal

Interpersonal intelligence affords those who have it the gift of understanding, appreciating, and getting along well with other people. This intelligence is not usually measured in the traditional academic setting, and those who possess it often find themselves in trouble for using it! These people have a sixth sense when it comes to reading another person. They can almost always tell when something's wrong, even if no words have been spoken. Those who need a friend are quickly drawn to the person with interpersonal intelligence.

One teacher admitted she did not keep traditional lesson plans. Her lesson plan book was, in fact, more of a *diary* where she recorded what she did, not what she planned. She had a general idea of what needed to be communicated, but she would wait to "get a sense" of where the students were on any given day before she determined how to proceed with the lesson.

Many of those in the helping professions such as counseling or ministry find themselves relying heavily upon their interpersonal abilities for success in their careers. Although you can work on developing this intelligence, it seems many remain very uncomfortable if they are not naturally gifted inter-personally.

Intrapersonal

Intrapersonal intelligence is not always readily apparent in a person because it so often expresses itself in solitude. It is a natural gift of understanding ourselves, knowing who and what we are, and how we fit into the greater scheme of the universe. Those who are naturally strong intrapersonally enjoy times of reflection, meditation, and time alone. They seem to possess a more positive self concept than most, and they don't rely on others' opinions to determine their life goals and aspirations.

A perfect example of intrapersonal intelligence is found in the book *The Accidental Tourist* by Anne Tyler. The main character, Macon, said of a woman friend that she talked too much. Macon, on the other hand, was the kind of man who thought silence was better than music. When his wife would switch off the radio, he'd say, "Listen! They're playing my song."

Sometimes we misunderstand those who excel in intrapersonal intelligence. We may accuse them of being introverted and shy, when those characteristics may actually be indicative of great inner strength.

In a Nutshell

No single test can ever measure or predict a person's intelligence. Everyone can win when given a chance to show *how* they are smart. The acceptance of a theory about multiple intelligences helps us value the differences among various world cultures. Although our culture may place a high value on linguistic intelligence, in some areas of the world, one's ability to read and write would take a back seat to spatial skills if you needed to navigate the seas to survive. The more we learn to identify and use multiple ways of being smart, the more effective our education system can become in equipping the next generation for dealing with the real world.

Chapter Eleven

Putting It All Together

I had just finished teaching two days of intensive learning and communicating styles training for a large police department. The police chief called me into his office to express his appreciation and to make an important request. He handed me a list of all his employees by name, including police officers, clerks, and other staff. "I'd like you to put each person's learning style category in the space beside his name," he said matter of factly.

I tried to hide the dismay I felt at his cut-and-dried categorization. However, I knew how *his* learning styles assessments had come out. So I said, "OK, let's start with *your* name. What style category should I put beside it?"

He thought for a moment. "I came out AR," he replied, "but actually, my CS was only a couple of points behind. And, truthfully, I am more analytic than global. And I'm definitely more visual."

I smiled. "So what shall I write beside your name?"

He frowned uncomfortably, then sighed. "OK, OK, I get your point. No *one* category can really describe anyone. But it would be so easy if I could just keep a file in my desk that lets me instantly figure out what style I'm dealing with!"

When we first discover this whole area of learning styles, there is a tendency to label everyone and everything according to one particular style, to categorize or put them in a box. But the more you understand about learning styles, the less you will try to categorize yourself and others. Each person is as unique as his or her fingerprints. Although many fingerprints may look basically the same, no one pattern is exactly like another. Sometimes the differences are hard to notice; at other times, they are quite obvious.

In this book, I have introduced you to five different learning styles models to help you understand that each person is a complex and unique combination of natural strengths and preferences. Let's quickly list them for review:

Mind-styles (Gregorc)

Recognizing how the mind works.

Environmental Preferences (Dunn and Dunn)

Designing the ideal study environment.

Modalities (Barbe-Swassing)

Learning strategies for remembering.

Analytic/Global Information Processing (Witkin)

Identifying effective methods of learning and study skills.

Multiple Intelligences (Gardner)

Identifying seven different areas of intelligences.

Each of these learning styles adds another dimension to our insights about ourselves and others in our families. In addition to these, there are literally hundreds of learning style models. The five I have chosen to share with you are my favorites, because I have seen firsthand how accurate and practical the results of these models can be, and because each has an extremely reliable research base. Now that you have become aware of these learning styles, you will encounter other means of identifying styles. Consider each model or test to be another layer of understanding and not a replacement for the labels you already know.

For many of us, no matter how many learning style assessments we take, we find our natural strengths and preferences to be very consistent with one another. For example, my random nature lives with my global style quite compatibly. I don't struggle to understand who I am or what I need in most situations. The obvious drawback to this consistency is that when I need to use the characteristics that are *opposite* my natural strengths, it takes a good deal of discipline and hard work, and I am left feeling frustrated and exhausted.

One of my best friends finds herself strongly random, but she is also very analytical. This causes her a great deal of conflict within herself. She needs structure and specific facts for analytic learning, but as a random communicator, she fights regimentation and detail. Once she began to understand about learning styles, she could use her seemingly contradictory traits to bring balance to her life. She practiced using her analytical side when she needed to be specific and switched to her random side when she needed to see the big picture.

Some people are frustrated that they never seem to fall into *any* definite category on any learning or communicating styles assessments. I usually suggest, lightheartedly, that they are either very well balanced or *really* mixed up! They are willing to admit they feel mixed up, but with a little more knowledge about and practice of learning styles, they usually begin to see the advantage of switching easily from style to style as circumstances dictate.

One of the most important things to remember about learning styles is that they are *value neutral*. There is no one best style to be. No single style is any smarter than another, nor is there any style combination that is automatically good or naturally bad. The key lies in how you *use* your natural style strengths, and in how willing you are to learn or communicate in a way that may be difficult for you.

USING LEARNING STYLES TO SURVIVE AND CONQUER!

Over my years of teaching learning styles to virtually all kinds of audiences, I have discovered a very consistent pattern in successfully understanding and using learning styles concepts and strategies. Both children and adults experience five stages in coming to fully understand them.

Stage One—Awareness

When we first discover the differences between the dominant learning styles perspectives, we enter the stage of awareness. There are a lot of "ah-ha's!" and enlightening revelations, and it is usually fun just to revel in being the "real" us. For many, it is both reassuring and, at the same time, unsettling to think that others actually *do* perceive the world as we do! Children who find learning difficult are especially delighted and encouraged to discover they are smart and capable after all, and they are usually eager to talk about what they like and how they learn best.

Stage Two—Opposite Camps

After the initial joy of discovery, the next stage can cause concern to those around us. When we look at the characteristics of those whose dominant style is opposite ours, we may decide our style is better than theirs. Without meaning to, we may even go so far as to insult those who are in opposite style groups.

Since children sometimes have a tendency to exaggerate the differences, adults may become alarmed when they hear the dominant globals or randoms referred to as "space cadets," or the dominant analytics or sequentials dubbed as "uptight nerds." A wise parent intervenes with gentle and consistent reminders that there is no best style, and each person's strengths are needed to keep the world in balance. This negative stage is just a normal part of the process of understanding learning styles. Fortunately, it doesn't last long.

Stage Three—Appreciation

After we have determined that we *like* our own natural style, we begin to realize some of our limitations. At that point, we come to appreciate the dominant styles that are opposite ours. We discover firsthand that each style has its strengths, and we can benefit from *all* of them. For example, when the more global students have been absent for two or three days and need to get notes or homework assignments from other students, it isn't a global classmate they ask for information. As much as they *like* their global friends, they search out their more *analytic* classmates who probably wrote down the assignment word for word and know every detail.

By the same token, dominant analytics often don't want to work in groups where everyone is analytic. For one thing, it seems that analytics often don't take into consideration how other people feel. They are all so interested in getting their point across that they are not always paying attention to how others are responding. Another problem with an all-analytic group is that nobody looks at the big picture They are all caught up in the details. Pretty soon participants are looking around saying, "We'd better find a couple of globals for our group." This is the appreciation stage in action, and it is where children and adults alike can begin to see that other styles have a lot to offer.

The Fourth Stage—Excuses

After the positive stage of learning to appreciate other styles comes a stage that is perhaps the hardest for parents and teachers to tolerate. They hear children say things like: "I'm a random—I don't do math," or "I'm analytic—I don't do groups."

Again, it is necessary to give firm, loving reminders that if we are using our learning style simply as an excuse, we have not yet learned how to use it to succeed. When we discover our strengths, we can then *use* them to conquer virtually *anything*. And once we've learned how to use our strengths to succeed, we will no longer *need* excuses!

Stage Five—Style Flex

Style flex happens when we can take our natural style strengths and consciously flex or bend them into other learning styles that don't make as much sense to us or are not as comfortable for us. It can be done and it's something we do on purpose. You may be surprised at how much easier it is to do a task that is opposite from what is natural for you when you can identify which parts cause the problem. At that point you can *deliberately* set out to overcome the difficulties.

Parents encounter the most resistance from children who do not understand *why* they are being asked to learn in a way that does not make sense to them. When forced to step out of their natural style even before they understand or accept what their own style *is*, they feel frustrated and inferior because they do not experience success. Once children are given the opportunity to identify and use their inherent learning style strengths, they begin to feel confident enough in their abilities to stretch out of their comfort zones and attempt tasks that are more difficult.

HELPING YOUR CHILD SUCCEED IN THE CLASSROOM

Sometimes parents feel strongly that their children would learn best if they were taught by teachers who shared the same basic learning style strengths. However, it may actually be better to learn from a teacher who presents information from an entirely different perspective. For example, a global teacher may give a broader view to an analytic child. A sequential teacher may bring order to a random-style learner.

There's no question about it—children must learn to get along with *many* different kinds of learning styles if they want to be successful in our diverse and changing world. What's important to remember is that your child must *want* to learn to get along with different styles and approaches. That motivation will be different for each child.

When speaking to students, I often try to illustrate the importance of accommodating styles other than their own so they will not be limited in their success. Here is one of those illustrations that seems to demonstrate the importance of accommodation:

Suppose you were going to live in a foreign country for two years. You don't plan to learn the language, and you plan to talk only to those who can speak English. Furthermore, you have no plans to change your life-style by adapting to native customs and habits. You've made up your mind to do only what is comfortable for you.

Now you could probably *survive*, but you're not going to have the same kind of experience that you could have if you were to take the time and effort to learn the native language and life-styles of the country. The same is true for you at school, at home, and later in your career. By learning to adapt to other styles, you will broaden your scope of influence and success.

In a Nutshell

One learning style can be almost as different from another as two foreign languages are from each other. As parents and teachers, if we can become "multilingual" in styles, we can teach our children to value many different perspectives without sacrificing their own. But most importantly, we can help our children be successful in *spite* of school and workplace systems as well as because of them.

Chapter Twelve

The Difference Between Between Learning Style and Learning Disability

Karen was a lively, mischievous first grader when her teacher and principal began to suggest that her parents have her screened for possible hyperactivity or Attention Deficit Disorder (A.D.D.). Even though Karen was bright and creative, they explained, she simply didn't follow directions. She was often restless and had difficulty staying at a task for more than five minutes at a time. She rarely completed written assignments, and her social interactions with her classmates were frequently immature and moody.

Karen's parents took her to a pediatrician. Subsequently, she went through an intensive screening process to determine whether or not she had a learning disability. The results of the testing led the doctor to conclude that Karen, indeed, had a marginal case of A.D.D. It was recommended that Karen begin a mild dose of medication to control her behavior.

Karen's parents and grandparents were troubled at the prospect of putting their bright, cheerful, six year old on serious and regular medication. They

151

began to explore other alternatives, and in the process, they heard about learning styles and how they affect study habits and behavior. As they began to understand Karen's natural learning style, they realized the way in which Karen learned was often not compatible with classroom demands.

For example, Karen is a very kinesthetic learner who thrives on movement combined with listening. The teacher wanted her to sit still. But her parents decided to try another approach. Instead of forcing Karen to be still and look at them when they were giving her directions, they decided to let her fidget, squirm, and look around. Then they checked to see if she had been listening and were amazed to find she could repeat what they had said almost word for word.

Karen's global nature made it possible for her to continually scan the environment, listening and paying attention to multiple voices and stimuli. Her dominantly random mind was constantly searching for alternatives and seeing possibilities not obvious to most people. Her CR characteristics made her very impatient when learning anything that didn't immediately interest her.

Her parents also discovered some emotional problems that seemed to explain Karen's sometimes immature behavior with her friends and classmates. These were addressed. Then, by helping Karen come to terms with her natural learning strengths, her parents and teacher helped her overcome many of her frustrations with the traditional classroom and learning demands. They didn't let Karen give up when something didn't make sense to her, and they encouraged her to use what came naturally to her. They challenged her to find ways she *could* be successful.

Karen's parents were wise in that they explored many alternatives for solving her difficulties with school. They made medication a last resort and not a quick fix. Although many children *do* benefit from a regimen of medication, I am encountering many teachers, physicians, and learning specialists who are concerned that far too many children are being rapidly and inappropriately labeled with A.D.D. or another disability and are being placed on medication too quickly.

Many students who are struggling in school simply have learning styles that are incompatible with the structure of the traditional classroom and academic demands. Sometimes concerned parents jump to a conclusion and believe their children may have learning disabilities or disorders of some kind because they lack success in school. To help their children succeed, parents can spend an inordinate amount of money and energy searching for programs and cures. What they need to do is take time to sort out how much of the problem might be attributable to an incompatibility of the child's learning style with the school's traditional method of teaching

Remember that a typical school classroom makes very definite learning style demands. A student is required to sit still (very difficult for the kinesthetic learner), learn quietly (not always easy for the auditory learner who needs to hear it aloud), work independently (often counter productive for the globals and ARs), and demonstrate knowledge sequentially (very frustrating for randoms and globals).

For children who possess learning styles that match academic demands, school does not normally present much of a problem. But when students find themselves at odds with school, they can become frustrated with both themselves and the system. Without a knowledge and understanding of learning styles, students often can't tell a teacher what works for them and what is difficult, nor can they develop effective strategies for coping with the opposite styles of either the teacher or the classroom.

There are more dimensions to consider. Many problems are beyond the scope of simple learning styles. Such things as family dysfunction, violence, emotional disorders, physical limitations, or chemical imbalance can affect a child's ability to learn. Often these problems require the service of medical and professional people and agencies. It is surprising to find out how much more effective the intervention of these professionals will be when we can identify the dominant learning styles of those who are *experiencing* the problems.

It is important to understand that even the best programs and approaches can work *backwards* if there isn't a significant match between the learning styles of the child and the style of the program designed to help him. If you can help your children discover and use methods that work *with* their natural style strengths instead of against them, you may find them succeeding more than you ever thought possible.

After reading this book, you already know a lot more about the individual learning styles of your children. But if you find your child in need of professional intervention, you can begin to ask some important questions of those who offer programs to help him or her. If you know your child is more sequential, does the program offer a simple, logical structure? If your child is random, does the program offer flexibility and a personal approach?

In my work with pediatricians and learning specialists, I have found the most effective professionals are those who are committed to a balanced approach when dealing with learning difficulties. This approach takes into consideration a child's dominant learning styles as well as other factors such as mental, emotional, or physical disabilities.

Physical limitations do exist in some children, and I am grateful we have so many well-qualified and dedicated specialists to diagnose and treat these ailments. I would, however, encourage parents of struggling children to take down the lines of first defense. Before we take any drastic actions or interventions, we need to devote time and energy toward really getting to know and understand our children as individuals. We must not be too quick in assuming that the child's misbehavior or annoying habits are symptoms of a learning disorder. Sometimes we, parents, focus on how we would like our children to *act* more than what we want our children to *accomplish*. But if we focus more on *outcomes* and less on *methods*, we may find our children succeeding in ways that have never occurred to us. As you define what you are trying to get the child to do or learn—the desired result—and not on the process by which he learns, you may discover some very reasonable alternatives to traditional approaches.

Here are just a few examples of troublesome behaviors that often give parents reason to believe their child has a learning problem, when actually the behaviors may be an indication of learning styles that are incompatible with the demands being made.

The Problem

The child is restless; he will not sit still.

What Do You Need to Accomplish?

I need for him to listen attentively to the story being read.

An Alternative

Give him the option of sitting on the floor or changing positions discreetly, as long as he does not distract those around him. Hold him accountable for being able to relate the facts or main idea of the story.

What Do You Need to Accomplish?

I need for him to understand the concept being taught.

An Alternative

Have him explain the concept to a parent, a teacher, or a classmate, either verbally or in written form.

What Do You Need to Accomplish?

I need for him to follow verbal directions.

An Alternative

Have him repeat back what he heard to check his understanding of the directions.

What Do You Need to Accomplish?

I need for him to not distract the other children around him.

An Alternative

Challenge him to come up with creative ways to move around without bothering anyone. For example, could he doodle, take notes, move his feet quietly?

Combining the Alternatives for a Restless Child

A primary teacher found out for herself how much difference it could make in classroom management if she simply defined her outcomes. She had been struggling with a fidgety, strong-willed boy who refused to sit in his seat and listen to the story she was reading. In frustration, she stopped for a moment and asked herself, "What's the point? What do I need to accomplish here? Do I need him to sit in this chair, or do I need him to listen to the story?" She then gave him the option of sitting anywhere he wanted as long as he listened quietly to the story and did not disturb others around him. To her amazement, he immediately complied by sitting in the back of the room on the floor and giving her his full attention.

The Problem

The child will not complete assignments.

What Do You Need to Accomplish?

I need for him to finish what he starts.

An Alternative

Help him break up the assignment into smaller, more manageable pieces. Don't insist that the whole task be done in one sitting, but hold him accountable for all the parts.

What Do You Need to Accomplish?

I need for him to prove he knows the material.

An Alternative

Challenge him that if he can maintain a minimum score (i.e. 92 or higher) on each test, he only has to do as much of each homework assignment he feels is necessary to master the concept.

Combining the Alternatives for Getting a Child to Complete Assignments

Sarah was a bright, capable fifth grader who, after excelling in math during the first half of the year, suddenly decided to quit doing her math homework. Sarah's teacher and parents were concerned. Homework counted for a substantial portion of the semester grade, and now Sarah's normally excellent grade point average seemed to be in jeopardy.

I was called in to talk to Sarah to discover what might have caused this abrupt change in her behavior, as well as what might motivate her to start turning in her homework again. It didn't take long for Sarah to tell me why she no longer did her homework.

"It's too boring," she explained simply. "I hate having to do 20 problems when I understand how to do the process after doing five of them. I just decided it wasn't worth the trouble."

"Can you pass the math tests without any trouble?" I asked.

"Oh, sure," she replied. "I always get As on my tests."

After some discussions with Sarah, her parents, and her teacher, we came up with a workable solution. Sarah agreed to do at least half of her homework every night. If she got a 92 percent or better on her math test, her teacher would give her full credit for the homework assignments. If she got lower than 92 percent, she would agree to complete whichever assignments her teacher deemed necessary.

Sarah kept her end of the bargain. Some nights she did *more* than half of the homework, because now she knew she was only doing what she needed to do in order to master the concept. She never did fall below a 92 percentile on any math test the rest of the year.

The Problem

The child won't stay at a task for more than a few minutes.

What Do You Need to Accomplish?

I need for him to learn to focus on one thing at a time.

An Alternative

Provide him with some options. Decide what needs to be done, then offer one or two ways to do it. Let him switch ways in the middle if he wants to, and let him keep on the move whenever possible while doing the task. Insist he do only one thing at a time, even if he quickly switches from one task to another. Help him identify which method he is using each time he changes direction.

What Do You Need to Accomplish?

I need for him to do it *my* way!

An Alternative

As parents, we have to admit that sometimes it's just plain easier for us if our children will do it our way. Try explaining to your child *why* you think your way will work, then offer to let your child try another method as long as he can prove his way will accomplish the same goal. The hardest part of this suggestion is the patience and tolerance it may take on your part to let your child try out the alternatives!

Combining the Alternatives for Getting a Child to Stay at a Task

I received a letter several years ago from a mother who attended one of my seminars. It remains one of my very favorites because it illustrates how one mom discovered the value of letting her son choose his own way to accomplish a goal. This mother writes:

> Style awareness has changed our lives. I look for ways to have Dan be creatively successful. We have a small farm, and

Dan has an acre he has begrudgingly taken care of for four years. He waters with a hose and sprinkler. It's a real pain, and he tells me so regularly. I suggested he brainstorm solutions to the watering problem and then make a list of the five ways he thought he could do better. He would then "sell" his choice to me. We have two greenhouses (25' x 50') we no longer use. He suggested a water system using salvaged plastic pipe from the greenhouses. I thought it was a great idea, provided (a) he could do it with materials we had, and (b) it would wet the whole garden all at once or in sequence. I suggested he play with hoses and sprinklers to see what the pump capacity was. He's 11 years old. He agreed and worked at it for a week.

It took a whole week of devotion, commitment, and an expressed need for privacy. He used about six times the pipe I would have used, and I'm *sure* every T, union, plug, and clamp on the property. But he did it all by himself, and it *does* water the whole acre in three rotations. The middle set spells his name when the water comes on. The system is as unique as Dan!

Don't fall into the trap of believing your child is smart and successful only if he or she does well in the traditional classroom. There are *many* ways of being smart. If you as a parent can help your child discover areas of intelligence and then reinforce that intelligence, you help build your child's confidence and abilities more than you could ever have imagined. Even if you believe your child is suffering from a legitimate learning disability or disorder, you can greatly increase your child's chances of success by determining natural learning style strengths and deciding how much of his frustration and difficulty is a matter of learning style differences and how much is a genuinely physical or emotional problem.

David was an angry, rebellious 15 year old. His parents were at the end of their rope. They had had conferences with teachers, counseled with psychologists, conferred with medical specialists, and prayed with clergy. They had tried punishment, rewards, discussion, threats, and ultimatums. Instead of improving, David steadily become more out of control. When David ran away for the third time in six months and was arrested for shoplifting, his parents were ready to take drastic action. They arranged to have him involuntarily committed to a youth facility where he would be locked up 24 hours a day. There he would undergo a regimented program designed to instill respect and appropriate behaviors through strict authoritarian discipline.

Just before David's scheduled commitment, his parents attended my seminar about learning styles. When they heard about the strong-willed, Concrete Random style, they immediately recognized their son. As they discovered how the CR mind works and identified strategies for motivating and disciplining a CR, their approach with David began to change. During the last seminar session when they were asked how they were doing with David, they made a statement that startled the rest of the group.

"Last night we asked David to forgive us." They went on to explain. "We told him we were sorry for not taking into account his *design*. We don't apologize for the outcomes we've expected, but we realize now that we could have handled many situations in ways that respected how his mind works. We could have helped him know how valued he is as a member of our family."

In the days and weeks that followed, David's parents talked to him about bottom lines, about outcomes and consequences. Then they gave David the opportunity to tell them what *he* could live with and what he couldn't. With the help of an understanding counselor, they are beginning a healing process that will make them a family again.

David realizes that he still must pay the consequences for his rebellion and criminal behavior. Although the youth facility is a very effective program for some styles, David's parents recognized that the program's approach would likely work backwards for David's style. With David's input and the counselor's help, they have found a rehabilitation program that makes sense to his CR nature. Progress is slow and sometimes painful, but David and his parents are convinced that recognizing and appreciating different styles is helping them put their family back together again.

So much of what we parents perceive as our children's deliberate attempts to annoy and frustrate us are actually a difference in approach and perspective. If we can learn to discern what is a learning style difference and how much is true disobedience or defiance, we will be much wiser parents.

I was conducting a seminar at a retreat for day-care teachers and staff. We had divided the group into randoms and sequentials, and I asked both groups the same question.

"If you could never have another raise in pay, what could your organization do to keep you happily working?"

The answer was almost unanimous: "Don't make us work with any 'difficult children.' "

When I asked them to define the "difficult child," the contrast between the groups was very evident. The sequential teachers claimed that the difficult children were those who were so random that they couldn't seem to follow the simplest directions. These children were spontaneous, unpredictable, and often disorganized.

The random teachers disagreed with the others. They claimed that difficult children were the more sequential ones. They were picky and structured, and they never seemed to "lighten up." These sequential children demanded predictable schedules and prompt attention to detail.

In the end, we all came to the same important conclusion. There really isn't a definitive "difficult child." The child who is most difficult is the one who doesn't think like we do!

In a Nutshell

We have spent quite a bit of time in this book trying to identify the consistent patterns of individual learning styles. Although we can learn to accommodate many of those styles, we'll never really be able to neatly label or categorize anyone. Because each human being is so complex, we may never fully appreciate all our differences.

It's never been more important to help our children succeed in a world that is often difficult to understand. It can make a difference with *your* children if you will devote time and energy to discovering *the way they learn.*

Endnotes Book I

Chapter Two

1. Order the *Adult Style Delineator* from Anthony F. Gregorc, 15 Doubleday Rd, Columbia, Connecticut 06237.

Chapter Seven

1. Kenneth and Rita Dunn are the authors of several books (see bibliography) and editors for *Learning Styles Network*. Contact: The Center for the Study of Learning Styles, St. John's University, Jamaica, N.Y.

Chapter Eight

1. *The Swassing-Barbe Modality Index*. Administered individually, 20 minutes, all ages, patterns are presented in each modality and must be retained and repeated. Available from Zaner-Bloser, Inc., Columbus, Ohio.

Chapter Nine

1. Herman A. Witkin, "Cognitive Styles in the Educational Setting," *New York University Education Quarterly*, 1977, pp. 14-20.

   Herman A. Witkin et. al.,"Field Dependent and Field-Independent Cognitive Styles and Their Educational Implications," *Review of Educational Research*, Winter 1977, vol. 47, No. 1, pp. 1-64.

Dedication

This book is dedicated to my parents,
Robert and Minnie Ulrich. Although they had
every reason to be frustrated with me—their headstrong,
restless, unpredictable daughter—their love, patience,
and encouragement brought out the best in me.
Their example is the best legacy
I can pass on to my own children.

Acknowledgments

*I would like to gratefully acknowledge my husband, John,
for his tireless support as working husband and Mr. Mom;
my treasured friends and colleagues Carol Funk and Kathy Koch, for
their invaluable advice and critique; my secretary and dear friend
Darlene Fleutsch, for her dedication and zeal; and Gwen Ellis,
my first editor, for taking my talent and inspiring me
to become a writer.*

Table of Contents

Preface

For every parent who has experienced frustration with his or her children, I believe this book will provide some of the best advice you'll ever get. In order to get the most out of what you're about to read, however, it's important to keep in mind the following two statements:

1. **Often the characteristics and behaviors that annoy us most about our children will be the qualities that make them successful as adults.** You may feel your child talks too much or moves too much or takes too many chances, and yet those are some of the traits that are consistently found in successful entrepreneurs and business leaders. Although you must maintain bottom-line accountability and discipline, remember that the children who may be most inconvenient for you now may, when they grow up, turn out to be the best thing that ever happened to this world.

2. **The quality of the relationship you have with each child will determine the effectiveness of the techniques you use.** If you have cultivated a loving and healthy relationship with each of your children, they will care very much about preserving it. If there is no benefit in keeping the parental relationship intact, your efforts to discipline and motivate may have little or no effect. Even the child with the strongest will responds more to love and genuine kindness than to creative or flashy methods and approaches.

Much of what you read in this book will validate what you've believed in your heart all along. I did not make up any of these concepts; they're all based on solid, empirical research. As you read these pages, you'll come to realize that both you *and* your children are unique and wonderful individuals with great strengths and promise.

Enjoy this book. It may be the best thing that has happened to your family in a long time.

Chapter One

How Can Such a Wonderful Kid Cause So Much Stress?

"Why can't you just do what you're told?"
"*Look* at me when I'm talking to you!"
"This room is a *mess!*"
"You just don't appreciate what you have."
"Kids! They think they know it all—you can't tell them *anything!*"
"You'd better watch your attitude!"

As a parent, you know that each of your children is a God-given gift with special talents and unique and wonderful characteristics. But let's face it—the same child who gives you so much joy can also be your greatest challenge. In fact, you may have noticed that every child in your family presents a *different* challenge. How can children growing up in the same home with the same parents be so diverse? Why don't your children automatically deal with the world in the same way you do? Do they *deliberately* annoy you? Are they *trying* to drive you crazy?

Over the years, researchers have discovered many of the reasons each person is unique. There are so many pieces to this puzzle that for some people, the issue has become too complex. Researchers have identified several personality types, at least four different temperaments, and many diverse management and teaching styles.

If it sounds overwhelming, it can be. But this book is here to offer you hope. Most busy parents, even when motivated, can't spare the time to delve into ponderous academic literature, only to find they'll have to dig out any practical nuggets for themselves. Ironically, many researchers of individual differences seem convinced that their model is the only one a person would need. Therefore, as you study a researcher's work and approach, you'll feel a need to "fit" yourself neatly into one of the categories. Even when the research and methods are sound, many who try to understand the theory give up in frustration when it comes to putting it into practice.

In my first book, *The Way They Learn*, I introduced five different research models in the field of learning styles—inborn strengths and characteristics possessed by every individual.[1] If personality and temperament are some of the most significant portions of each person's puzzle, then learning styles are the pieces that make up the border. (See puzzle diagram on p. 24.) Your learning style determines what makes sense to you, what's most important, and what you need in order to fully understand and communicate information.

Shortly after *The Way They Learn* was released, a junior high school in the state of Washington received some grant money for a project to help its Learning Assistance Program (LAP). Although the students in this program were all struggling in school, they weren't eligible for special education funds or instruction. Many of these seventh, eighth, and ninth graders were failing numerous academic subjects, and several were bordering on juvenile delinquency. One teacher, Mrs. Troy,* had chosen to become a full-time instructional aide in order to work with these particular kids. She was also completing her certification as a learning styles specialist. Together we sat down and designed a program that would enable the LAP students to discover and use their learning style strengths to improve their performance in school, as well as to boost confidence in their ability to succeed in life. The school purchased a copy of *The Way They Learn* for each student in the program,

---

*Names have been changed.

and Mrs. Troy was able to use both formal (research-validated) and informal (abbreviated, nonscientific) instruments for assessing the students.

Mrs. Troy was tireless in her efforts, and she single-handedly spent six weeks assessing each of the more than 80 students, helping them pinpoint their dominant learning style strengths in all five of the research models used in the book. I conducted several hours' worth of instruction for the school staff and spoke to interested parents at a PTA program.

The response of the students was overwhelmingly positive. They were flattered that an adult would even *ask* about how they learn. They couldn't imagine that a teacher would actually *want* to develop alternative strategies for studying and learning. Although there were many success stories, one of my favorites is about Jake, a ninth grader who had one foot in the principal's office and the other foot in Juvenile Hall.

Mrs. Troy was determined to get to Jake. He was failing every subject and hadn't done any homework for almost a year and a half. "He's a great kid," insisted Mrs. Troy. "He's bright and capable, and he has a wonderful sense of humor. These grades do *not* reflect what Jake can do." After determining Jake's dominant learning styles, she set up a conference with him.

At first, Jake appeared disinterested in the results of his learning styles assessments. Mrs. Troy picked up a copy of *The Way They Learn* and pushed it across the desk to him.

"This is your book, Jake," she said.

He grinned and shook his head. "Oh no, Mrs. Troy. I don't *read* books."

She persisted. "The book is yours. I'd like you to just look through it," she said.

He shrugged, picked up the book, and walked out.

A few days later, Mrs. Troy received an urgent message in her mailbox in the faculty room. Jake's mother wanted to talk to her right away. With some reluctance and a certain amount of dread, Mrs. Troy called. Jake's mother insisted she come and have a conference in person, so Mrs. Troy arranged to meet with her that afternoon.

Jake's mom was almost breathless when she met with Mrs. Troy. She started talking right away. "I don't know what you've done to my son," she began. "The other day he came home with this book." She held up Jake's copy of *The Way They Learn*. "He said, 'Mom, you've got to read this book! This is *me* in this book!' Then he made his father and me sit down at the kitchen table while he went through all the various learning style descriptions you talked to him about. He kept pointing out the ones that fit him. I've never seen him so excited about something he did at school."

Mrs. Troy smiled, but before she could speak, Jake's mom said, "Here's the best part. Yesterday we were all going to go shopping for school supplies, and Jake asked if we would wait for him while he did his English homework. I almost fainted! We waited, and he finished every bit of homework for the first time in *months!*" She leaned closer, and Mrs. Troy could see her eyes brimming with tears. "I don't know what you've done, but my son is a different boy. Tell me how to make this last!"

Mrs. Troy was able to help Jake's mom, along with dozens of other parents, develop practical strategies to work with their children's learning style strengths. There are plans to continue and expand this program every year for all the students in the school, since many of them begged to be tested for learning styles even though they weren't in the program. The students are excited about the possibilities.

Learning styles is certainly not a magic formula or quick answer to all our problems. But it provides an invaluable framework that can enable us as parents and educators to focus on individual strengths and begin to build confidence within our children for becoming successful, lifelong learners. With our knowledge of learning styles, we can provide parents and teachers with a more detailed road map than we currently distribute through standard school systems. We need to keep finding *many* ways to help our children be successful, and the strategies in the following chapters will give you lots of fuel for the journey.

You will find that this book, while it offers invaluable advice and diverse strategies, holds true to the concept of accountability and high standards of conduct. I do not endorse letting children rely on their learning styles as an excuse, or using their "style" to get away with inappropriate behaviors.

Many adults have grown up feeling that they are not really as smart as everyone else. More and more children are finding that they just don't fit into the traditional education system. Because of our research in learning styles, we have discovered and documented that there are *many* ways of being smart. Each of us was created as a unique and gifted individual. Even those born with severe physical limitations have been endowed with some wonderful gifts and abilities. What a relief it has been for literally thousands of people of all ages to discover that they really do possess capabilities and areas of strength.

As you read this book, you will find that most of what you discover will be helpful for you in understanding *yourself* as well as your children. Keep an open mind as you read, and try to be as flexible as possible when it comes to helping your children succeed by using their learning style strengths. I believe you'll be amazed at the difference your knowledge and use of learning styles will make, both within your own family and among your colleagues at work. You may even discover that the things about your children that frustrate you most are actually some of their greatest strengths and abilities.

Plan of Action

Keep a brief journal of your interactions with and observations of each of your children. If you don't want to make entries daily, do so weekly. Use the following questions as guidelines.

1. What made_____(child's name) happiest this week?

2. What frustrated him/her?

3. What conversation between the two of us this week stands out in my mind? Why?

4. What new approach have I tried with _____this week? How did it work?

5. Which of _____'s strengths really stood out this week?

6. What do I know about_____that I didn't know a week ago?

Chapter Two

Parents, Do *Your* Homework First!

You're probably reading this book because you want to find ways to help your children be happy and successful. You want them to achieve in school and become lifelong learners. Before you can help your children, however, you need to understand your own learning style strengths. That's where this chapter's assignment comes in—perhaps the most important homework you *or* your child will ever do.

The following account from Max Lucado's *In the Eye of the Storm* illustrates the importance of parents doing their *own* homework before expecting their children to complete their assignments.

> February 15, 1921. New York City. The operating room of the Kane Summit Hospital. A doctor is performing an appendectomy.
>
> In many ways, the events leading to the surgery are unevent-

ful. The patient has complained of severe abdominal pain. The diagnosis is clear: an inflamed appendix. Dr. Evan O'Neill Kane is performing the surgery. In his distinguished thirty-seven-year medical career, he has performed nearly four thousand appendectomies, so this surgery will be uneventful in all ways except two.

The first novelty of this operation? The use of local anesthesia in major surgery. Dr. Kane is a crusader against the hazards of general anesthesia. He contends that a local application is far safer. Many of his colleagues agree with him in principle, but in order for them to agree in practice, they will have to see the theory applied.

Dr. Kane searches for a volunteer, a patient who is willing to undergo surgery while under local anesthesia. A volunteer is not easily found. Many are squeamish at the thought of being awake during their own surgery. Others are fearful that the anesthesia might wear off too soon.

Eventually, however, Dr. Kane finds a candidate. On Tuesday morning, February 15, the historic operation occurs.

The patient is prepped and wheeled into the operating room. A local anesthetic is applied. As he has done thousands of times, Dr. Kane dissects the superficial tissues and locates the appendix. He skillfully excises it and concludes the surgery. During the procedure, the patient complains of only minor discomfort.

The volunteer is taken into post-op, then placed in a hospital ward. He recovers quickly and is dismissed two days later.

Dr. Kane had proven his theory. Thanks to the willingness of a brave volunteer, Kane demonstrated that local anesthesia was a viable, and even preferable, alternative.

But I said there were two facts that made the surgery unique. I've told you the first: the use of local anesthesia. The second is the patient. The courageous candidate for the surgery by Dr. Kane was Dr. Kane.

To prove his point, Dr. Kane operated on himself!

A wise move. The doctor became a patient in order to convince the patient to trust the doctor.[1]

The lesson to be drawn from the preceding story is that before you can pinpoint your children's strengths and preferences, you first must know and understand your own. For one thing, it'll give you insight into why you and your children experience many of the conflicts you do. Also, the way you perceive and deal with information will largely determine the expectations you have for your children. Finally, and perhaps most important, as your children see the difference understanding learning styles makes in *your* life, it will be natural for them to follow your example.

In the next few pages, you'll find a brief review of the five different learning styles models I first introduced in *The Way They Learn*.[2] As you work your way through the descriptions, try to identify your own strengths and preferences. You'll find that you won't fit neatly into any one category and that there are no all-or-nothing methods of recognizing particular learning styles. As you proceed with the general learning styles profile, you'll also be able to consider the strengths of each of your children. Bear in mind that this is not a formal assessment; it is simply a quick and painless way to begin using learning styles to design effective strategies for helping your children be successful, happy, and productive.

GENERAL LEARNING STYLES PROFILE

Environmental Preferences (How Do You Concentrate?)

Researchers Kenneth and Rita Dunn have provided us with hundreds of studies showing how important it is to recognize and use natural learning style strengths when it comes to where, when, and how we study and learn effectively.[3] Not all of the following elements will have the same importance to you, but you'll find them helpful in identifying what kind of environment you need to concentrate best.

Time of Day

After decades of various research projects, scientists have confirmed what most of us have known all along: Each of us has certain times of the day or night when we simply can't be at our best. That doesn't mean we don't learn to cope, but it *does* give us important information about ourselves when it becomes essential that we *really* concentrate.

Think about the time of day when you are naturally more productive. Are you an early morning person or a night owl? Are there consistent times during the day when you find your mind drifting? Have you learned to avoid doing your most difficult tasks at your least effective time of day?

Each child will also exhibit some of these preferences early in life. One will wake up at the crack of dawn, while the other has to be dragged out of bed. One will be dozing on the couch by 6:00 P.M., while the other will be climbing the walls. What we often don't realize is that we can help our children use their time most productively by working *with* their internal clocks instead of against them. For example, I've always been a morning person. The *worst* time for me to do my homework was in the evening. Even now I'm usually better off getting up early (often hard to do, even for the morning person!) and doing my most difficult tasks while I'm fresh and enthusiastic about my day. My husband, on the other hand, can really produce results doing tasks between 9:00 P.M. and 2:00 A.M. and is pretty worthless until about 10:00 A.M. the next day. Naturally, we seem to have produced a son in each category!

Where would you put the mark that indicates *your* best time of day?

Early Bird   Night Owl

Intake

I discovered long ago that I almost never got my best work done unless I had something to eat and/or drink while I was concentrating. As an adult, I usually have a cup of coffee handy, as well as a healthy snack for nibbling. When it comes to our children, however, we often don't take into account their need for nutritional intake while they're doing homework or trying to pay attention in class. Although it's not always possible to let your children eat or drink while they're studying, you may be surprised at the increase in learning that takes place when you don't make eating or drinking an issue.

How would you rate your own need for intake?

Eat or Drink to Think   Can't Think While Eating or Drinking

Light

As you're reading this book, what kind of light are you using? If you're one who needs a brightly lit room or study space, chances are good that you insist your children do the same. If you prefer softer illumination, you may actually cringe when you walk into a room flooded with light. As long as a person can comfortably see, there *is* no standard level of light that is necessary for everyone.

Which level of light is comfortable for you?

___

Bright   Soft or Dim

Design

Have you ever walked into your child's bedroom expecting to find her studiously doing her homework at that student desk you paid good money for, only to find both her and her books and papers spread over the bed and floor? Does your child prefer draping over the chair in the living room to sitting quietly at the kitchen table? When it comes to the design of the room or study area, individual preferences are almost always unique. If you prefer to sit at a desk, you can usually expect to have at least one child who prefers the opposite. The question is, does the work get done?

What design do you find yourself gravitating toward when you really have to study or concentrate?

___

Formal (desk, chair, etc.)   Informal (couch, floor, etc.)

Temperature

It's no coincidence that dual controls on electric blankets are more popular than single controls. Although most of us can adapt to various climates when necessary, we usually have a particular temperature range at which we work best. For many children, temperature may not be that important. But for those who can't concentrate unless the room feels comfortable, this may be a more critical issue than you thought.

What about you? What should the temperature be for you to work at your best?

___

Cold   Hot

Modalities (How Do You Remember?)

Modalities is the word we use to describe the various modes of remembering. According to the Walter Barbe–Raymond Swassing model, when you need to remember information, you use at least three basic modes: auditory (hearing), visual (seeing), and kinesthetic (moving).[4] Although each of us uses all three, we often benefit most when we're employing our strongest method.

Auditory

When you need to think, does it help to talk through your thought process? Do you frequently find yourself talking aloud even when no one else is in the room? If your auditory mode is strongest, you need to actually hear yourself *say* what you need to remember. When you are helping your child study, a more auditory learner may really thrive with verbal drill and repetition. Interestingly, strong auditory people, more than others, may need silence while working or concentrating because of how easily other noises distract them.

How strong are your auditory preferences?

Most Preferred   Least Preferred

Visual

Have you ever been listening to someone speak and suddenly found yourself struggling to picture what in the world they're talking about? You may be accused of daydreaming or tuning out when what you were really doing was trying to get a visual handle on the information you need to remember. When you use your visual modality, you will usually find yourself highlighting as you read, or color coding notebooks or files. A strongly visual child is almost always helped by visual aids such as flash cards, pictures, and charts.

When you're dealing with an extremely visual person, you can talk until you're blue in the face and simply be met with a blank stare—until you illustrate what you're saying!

How visual are you?

Very Visual   Not Visual

Kinesthetic

Have you ever been accused of being restless? Do you work best in short spurts? Is some part of your body in almost constant motion? If you answered yes to any of these questions, the chances are good that you are kinesthetic. Simply put, you need to keep moving in order to focus and concentrate on learning and remembering information. For highly kinesthetic children, school is often torture when they have to sit still without a break for long periods. Kinesthetic children will usually learn more by *not* always having to sit still, because they aren't distracted by the lure to get up and move!

How kinesthetic are you?

Very Kinesthetic   Not Kinesthetic

Cognitive Style (How Do You Interact with Information?)

The Herman Witkin model of learning styles helps us understand fundamental differences in the way each of us takes in and communicates information and how we communicate it to others.[5]

Those who are more *analytic* by nature automatically break down the information coming in so that they can deal with it in smaller, component parts. They can focus easily on specific facts, but they may consider the bigger picture to be irrelevant until all the details are understood.

Those who are more *global* tend to be better at grasping the overall situation, getting the gist of things, and assuming the details will fall into place after establishing the big picture.

Although each of us possesses both analytic and global strengths, our bent toward one over the other is especially noticeable when we study or learn. The analytic learner is often overwhelmed when information isn't given in a logical, step-by-step order with clear, specific directions. Global learners, on the other hand, are more easily frustrated by a detailed explanation or specific method without an overall idea of where they're going.

Where would you place yourself on the continuum?

Definitely Analytic   Definitely Global

Multiple Intelligences (How Do You Show You're Smart?)

The traditionally accepted IQ tests are not necessarily what we expect them to be. For generations, we've been led to believe that our scores on IQ tests are definite indicators of how smart we are and how successful we're going to be. The fact is, there are *many* ways of being smart, and IQ tests measure only a small portion of them. Howard Gardner's research uncovered at least seven different intelligences, many of which cannot be measured by standard IQ tests.[6] Although his Multiple Intelligences model is not specifically related to learning styles, it's an important part of the picture. Let's take a quick look at the various ways we can be brilliant!

Linguistic

Linguistic intelligence measures verbal abilities: reading, writing, speaking, and debating, with particular skills in word games and semantics.

How much linguistic intelligence do you feel you have?

High   Low

Logical-Mathematical

Logical-mathematical intelligence has to do with abilities in numbers, patterns, and logical reasoning. Scientists, mathematicians, and philosophers are typically high in this area of intelligence.

How high is your logical-mathematical intelligence?

High   Low

Spatial

Spatial intelligence is the ability to think in vivid mental pictures, restructuring an image or situation in your mind. It is, by the way, also what helps you "find Waldo" in the popular series of hidden pictures.

How does your spatial intelligence measure on the following scale?

High   Low

Musical

Musical intelligence often shows up best through a person's ability with rhythm and melody, as well as general appreciation for orchestration of sounds and words. You don't have to be a professional musician to possess musical intelligence.

How high is your musical intelligence?

High   Low

Bodily-Kinesthetic

Bodily-kinesthetic intelligence helps a person use his/her body skillfully. This intelligence is especially important for surgeons, actresses, artists, athletes, and so on. Though children with this intelligence often get into trouble at school for their constant, restless movement, it will probably benefit them in their careers.

How high is your bodily-kinesthetic intelligence?

High   Low

Interpersonal

Interpersonal intelligence gives a person the ability to intuitively understand and get along with all kinds of people. Almost a "sixth sense," it's essential for pastors, teachers, counselors, and others who help people through difficult times. If you are strong in this type of intelligence, others are drawn to you as a friend and confidant.

Where would you place yourself on this intelligence scale?

High   Low

Intrapersonal

Intrapersonal intelligence is often expressed best in solitude. This is a natural gift for understanding ourselves, for knowing who we are and why we do the things we do. It's usually exhibited more subtly than other types of intelligence and often is overlooked by the casual observer.

How self-smart are you?

High   Low

Mind Styles™ (How Do You Communicate What You Know?)

One of the most interesting and effective learning styles models comes from the research of Anthony F. Gregorc.[7] In his Mind Styles™ model, Gregorc gives us an organized view of how our minds work. We perceive, or take in information, in two ways: *Concrete*—using our five senses; and *Abstract*—using our intuition and imagination. We also order information and organize our lives in two ways: *Sequential*—in a linear, step-by-step manner; and *Random*—in chunks, with no particular sequence. These two ways of perceiving and ordering give us four learning style combinations. Everyone has and uses all four, but most of us are dominant in at least one or two. (See the chart on p. 22 for a more detailed description of the following learning styles.)

Concrete Sequential (CS)

When you're being Concrete Sequential, you are using your practical, predictable side. You're straightforward and down-to-earth. You're stable, reliable, and often provide the "anchor" for those around you.

How well does this describe you?

Definitely   Definitely Not

Abstract Sequential (AS)

Your Abstract Sequential traits show up best when you're being logical, methodical, and analytic. You take your time when making decisions, and one of your greatest assets is your ability to be objective.

How well does this describe you?

Definitely   Definitely Not

Abstract Random (AR)

The aspects of your style that are Abstract Random are what make you especially sensitive to and effective with people. Your spontaneous and flexible nature draws other people to you. You know intuitively what others need.

How well does this describe you?

Definitely   Definitely Not

Concrete Random (CR)

Your Concrete Random nature makes you curious, adventurous, and quick to act on your hunches. It's what drives you to keep changing, growing, and taking risks.

How well does this describe you?

Definitely   Definitely Not

SO, WHAT AM I?

These descriptions are intended to be a brief introduction and/or review. For more details about each of these models, be sure to read my book *The Way They Learn*. Also, if you would like a quick and informal survey designed to help you talk to your children about identifying their learning styles, see the appendixes at the back of the book. Remember, your learning style strengths are pieces of a puzzle, not a neat category you can identify and fit into. You'll discover that recognizing these patterns and preferences will help you communicate more effectively with your children and others around you.

Every parent has an absolutely vital "home" work assignment: *Know your child!* Working your way through this chapter is a giant step toward better understanding your children (and yourself!) by identifying strengths. As you begin to apply this knowledge in the following chapters, keep in mind that each of us possesses unique and wonderful traits and characteristics. Even when yours don't match your child's, you can have a new and profound appreciation for the differences. Didn't you think your homework would be *harder* than this?

Four Combinations

Concrete Sequential (CS)

hardworking

conventional

accurate

stable

dependable

consistent

factual

organized

Abstract Sequential (AS)

analytic

objective

knowledgeable

thorough

structured

logical

deliberate

systematic

Abstract Random (AR)

sensitive

compassionate

perceptive

imaginative

idealistic

sentimental

spontaneous

flexible

Concrete Random (CR)

quick

intuitive

curious

realistic

creative

innovative

instinctive

adventurous

Plan of Action

When it comes to determining learning and personality styles, you'll never fit neatly into any one category. Each of us has many pieces that make up the whole of who we are. The following illustration uses puzzle pieces to show how complex and varied we all are. Our learning style strengths provide an important framework, or border, to the puzzle. If you can, draw a quick diagram of your own personal puzzle.

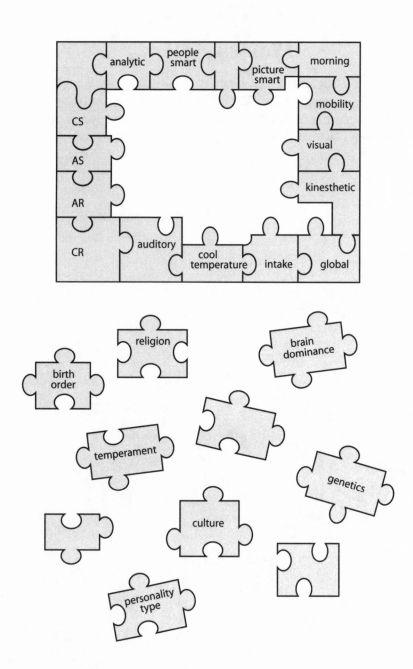

Chapter Three

Moving Them from Excuses to Accountability

"I'm a random—I don't do math."

"I'm a global—I don't *have* to have a clean room."

"I'm a kinesthetic learner—I *can't* sit still."

"I'm a sequential —I don't have to be flexible."

You've probably already heard enough excuses from your children to last a lifetime. So, what if helping your child discover learning styles creates a whole *new* set of excuses? Don't worry. Incorporating learning styles into your approach as a parent or teacher should never take the place of accountability. You don't have to sacrifice academic excellence or lower standards of behavior in order to accommodate a child's learning style strengths. But I do believe it's essential that we focus on what it is we want to accomplish in asking our children to do something. In other words, *what's the point?*

Remember that your *own* personal learning style will greatly influence how you perceive the learning styles of others, especially your children. For example, if you're sequential, your more random children may drive you crazy by their lack of organization. Are they giving you excuses because they don't want to do what you're asking, or do they simply need to find a way to accomplish the goal that makes sense to their styles? How can you tell the difference? I'd like to give you a few ideas about how you can hold your children accountable while still honoring individual learning strengths.

HOLDING YOUR CHILDREN ACCOUNTABLE

1. Define what needs to be accomplished or taught, and then find as many ways as possible to work with your child's learning style so he/she can master it. I remember listening to a local humorist a few years ago when he told about helping his daughter do homework. "I've finally figured out why I had to learn to multiply and divide fractions when I was in the fourth grade," he said. "It was so I could help my fourth-grade daughter do *her* homework!"

Some of the greatest battles fought in the home are over doing homework. Even the brightest and most cooperative kids often struggle with the discipline of this nightly ritual. Perhaps some of the best excuses ever heard have come from kids trying to get out of doing homework. As a teacher, I found I had to ask myself an important question: Why am I giving them these assignments?

Teachers and home-school parents may find the principle of clarifying the point of a task especially helpful in making instruction more effective. For years such things as multiplication tables, long division, sentence diagramming, and other fundamental methods of education have given children fits when they tried to master a vaguely defined concept. Why do you have to memorize multiplication tables? You do need to understand the concept of multiplication, but does everyone benefit from the same approach? Of course not. What's the point? If the point is to understand the mathematical concept in your head, then define your objective and meet it. If the point is that you should know how to do multiplication the long way in case you don't have a calculator handy, then be clear about what it is you're really trying to teach.

If you understand why you need to know what you're teaching your children, you can probably come up with alternative ways to teach the concept that are more compatible with their learning styles.

In *The Way They Learn*, I introduced my readers to a bright, young student named Sarah, who was failing math because she refused to do the homework.[1] Sarah was bored with the work, she said, because she hated doing 20 problems when she understood the concept after doing just three. Even though homework assignments counted for a third of Sarah's total grade, she decided it just wasn't worth it.

Fortunately, in Sarah's case, her teacher was extremely cooperative and open-minded, and he and Sarah struck a deal. Sarah agreed to do at least half of her math homework every night. If she got 92 percent or better on her math test, her teacher would give her full credit for all the lessons. If she got lower than 92 percent, she agreed to complete whichever assignments her teacher deemed necessary.

Sarah kept her end of the bargain. Some nights she did *more* than half of the homework, because now she knew she was doing only what was necessary for her to do well on the test. She never did fall below a 92 percentile on any math test the rest of the year.

Sarah's teacher caused a bit of a stir among the staff at the school. Questions came hard and fast: What if all the children wanted to try this approach? How in the world would you keep track of the various assignments? How would you be sure that every student was being treated equally?

You see, Sarah's teacher had asked himself the important question: What's the point? Since the point of doing the homework was to help his students understand the math concepts, he backed off from the standard requirement of completing every problem on the exercise sheet and began to help both himself *and* his students focus on why the homework was important. Granted, this approach took more time. He also found, however, that he was able to individualize many of his assignments with much less effort than he'd thought possible.

As parents and educators, we must take a good, hard look at why we assign homework. This issue is too important to simply keep using the task as a traditional form of discipline and study. Have we really done a good job of communicating with our students or children the purpose of what we assign?

Many students will complete the assignments simply because it fulfills a grade requirement. But what about the growing number of students who aren't motivated to do homework at all? For teachers and home-school parents especially, I would ask you to do this: If you believe in the importance of what you assign, either challenge yourself to prove to your students that the homework is doing them some good, or challenge the students to prove to you that they don't need to do the homework at all. For those students who recognize the purpose in the work but still believe it's too boring, challenge them to come up with alternative methods of achieving the goal. After all, they have a responsibility for meeting that outcome.

2. **Treating people equally does not mean treating them the same.**
"Hey, Mom! Charlie's changing everything around—that's not fair!"
"Well, do *you* want to do that?"
"No way! I just don't think it's fair that *he* gets to do it!"

Almost every parent who has more than one child struggles with issues of sibling rivalry, but utilizing each child's unique learning style may alleviate feelings of favoritism or unfairness. Since each of us is an individual, no single teaching method can be effective for everyone. My husband is my opposite in almost every area. If you were to insist that we both be taught in the *same* way when it comes to learning, one of us would be receiving very *unequal* treatment.

As you try to come up with compelling reasons for your children to do what they're told and not worry about their brothers or sisters, keep in mind *the bottom line*. "Look, Tim, the bottom line is this: You get to it one way; your brother gets to it another. The point is, you both accomplish the goal." It's important to teach your children as early as possible to honor the differences between them. If you effectively define the bottom-line outcomes, you'll be more effective in convincing them why treating everyone fairly means they aren't all treated exactly alike.

The traditional school system struggles with this concept because it takes much more time and effort to vary the methods for teaching objectives that often aren't clearly defined in the first place. It's simpler to just quantify everything and measure results by way of objective tests. If we continue to do this, we'll subject many of our children to an educational system that is more like a prison sentence than preparation for a successful, fulfilling life. There are no simple answers to this problem, but there is a simple question: What's the point?

3. **Stretching makes us stronger.** I remember as a child hearing my mother repeatedly say, "Well, I do a lot of things I don't feel like doing!" I would give her a puzzled look and say, "Why?" Most of us would prefer to do only what is convenient or comfortable for us, but it doesn't take long to figure out that the

rest of the world is not particularly anxious to cater to us. In fact, everyone who succeeds at work, school, and home *must* do things they don't like.

If the purpose of our children's education—both at home and at school—is to equip them to deal with life, then some of the most important lessons may be those that stretch them beyond their natural strengths and abilities and challenge them to think or learn in a different way. I believe the key lies in helping a child realize he/she is stretching on purpose. If we don't explain why something may be difficult for them, some children may just assume they're inadequate and so not even *try* to accomplish the task. If, on the other hand, they know where their strengths lie and as a result know what causes them frustration, they can start from a position of confidence and *deliberately* stretch out of what's comfortable.

As a classroom teacher, I often found that if I prefaced tasks with an explanation of what I was asking, my students were more successful. For example, I would say: "Now, this is going to seem a little vague and confusing for you sequentials who need a step-by-step explanation, but stick with me. I'm going to show you where the steps come in." I could see visible relief on the faces of those dominantly sequential students. *Whew!* they would say to themselves. *At least she knows this drives me crazy!* And usually it didn't bother them as much as they thought it would.

HOW MUCH IS A MATTER OF STYLE?

Parents shouldn't use *their* style as an excuse either. Often when we hear ourselves reply "Because I *said* so!" we're really insisting our children do it our way because it's more convenient than trying to figure out how to accomplish the same goal a different way. Other times, it's simply necessary that our children stretch out of what's comfortable for them and learn the discipline of doing what needs to be done.

When you experience conflict with your children, try to keep a perspective that allows you to decide how much of their behavior is due to a difference between your learning styles and how much is due to another cause (emotional, physical, etc.). Most of the time, neither parents nor children set about to deliberately annoy and frustrate each other. We do, however, feel most comfortable when other people do things in a way that makes sense to us, and that's where a knowledge and appreciation of learning styles is going to make a tremendous difference!

The chart on the following pages will help you identify some of the most common excuses used and give you some ideas for moving your children beyond them. As you read through the information, decide how you can hold your children accountable while still being true to their individual learning styles. When you're trying to decide whether or not your children are simply using excuses to avoid doing tasks, ask one important question: What's the point?

Excuses, Excuses!

What's Your Excuse?	Who Usually Gives It, and Why?	How Do We Move Them Beyond It?
"I'm too bored!"	*Concrete Randoms* (let's-just-get-this-over-with, how-much-is-necessary kids) They need compelling reasons to learn or pay attention.	If you or their teacher can't make things interesting for them, challenge them to learn how to motivate themselves.
	Analytics/ Abstract Sequentials (how-do-you-know-this, what-makes-you-the-expert kids) They may have lost respect for your credibility or authority. The task may be too easy to be challenging.	Establish credibility early on, and make sure they know where the facts come from. Let them do some of the research and documentation; be sure to recognize their efforts and input.
"The teacher doesn't like me!"	*Abstract Randoms/ Globals* (why-can't-everyone-just-get-along, we're-people-too kids) School and learning must be an intensely personal experience in order to have a lasting effect.	Work on noticing something positive about them as many times as possible during the day. When they work with a teacher who may be more analytic or sequential, help the students understand that just because the teacher forgets to be more global or random doesn't mean the teacher doesn't like them.

Excuses, Excuses!

What's Your Excuse?	Who Usually Gives It, and Why?	How Do We Move Them Beyond It?
"I left my books at school!"	*Globals/Randoms* *(out-of-sight-out-of-mind, I-meant-to-bring-it-home kids)* They had too many things to think about at the end of the schoolday.	Consider buying a second set of textbooks and leaving one set at home and one at school. Set a specific time and/or place each schoolday where they get together with a partner and quickly list what they need to take home.
"I never have time to finish my assignments!"	*Analytics/ Abstract Sequentials* *(if-there's-not-time-to-do-it-right-I-won't-do-it-at-all, why-are-you-in-such-a-hurry kids)* They need to work through an assignment thoroughly; they need to have clear and specific directions.	Be sure they understand the purpose of the assignment, as well as the reason for the stated deadline. If they need more time, give it to them, as long as you know they are truly working as well as they can. Help them get a "jump start" so they will not agonize over how to begin the assignment.

Excuses, Excuses!

What's Your Excuse?	Who Usually Gives It, and Why?	How Do We Move Them Beyond It?
"I just can't do my math!"	*Globals* *(just-get-the-gist-of-it,* *what's-the-big-deal kids)* They view math concepts as often overwhelming and rarely personal.	Help them break the concept down into manageable and understandable pieces; break down the assignment whenever possible. Use as many personal examples as possible.
	Randoms *(why-do-I-have-to-follow-the-steps,* *what's-the-point-anyway kids)* It's often impossible to show their work because they honestly don't know how they got the answer.	Help them apply the math problems in as many situations as possible instead of insisting on a step-by-step sequence, thereby demonstrating they understand the concept.
"I can't concentrate!"	*Analytics/Sequentials* *(give-it-to-me-one-at-a-time,* *just-stick-to-the-point kids)* They need to focus on one thing at a time and usually can't concentrate while others are talking or interrupting.	Help them keep their work space clutter-free; challenge them to practice working with distractions on less important assignments. Keep household interruptions to a minimum.
	Globals/Randoms *(hey-what's-everybody-doing,* *how-soon-do-we-do-something-* *else kids)* They are easily distracted by interesting activities or conversations.	Let them choose a more analytic/sequential partner who will gently help them keep focused.

Plan of Action

Which excuses do you hear most in your household? Can you think of reasons these excuses are given? What can you do this week to help your child move beyond them?

Chapter Four

What's It Going to Take to Motivate?

She was a bright and capable teenager who had just flunked out of math for the third time. I asked her the question her frustrated parents were desperate to know: "Why did you fail math *this* time?"

She shrugged and smiled grimly. "Because my parents told me 'No way are you going to flunk math again this semester.'"

Obviously, this method of motivating her had *not* had the desired effect!

What do you do when you know your child is achieving far below his/her potential? How do you motivate a procrastinator to start and finish a task? How can you get your children to do what they're told without constantly raising your voice or issuing threats? As you probably know, there are no simple answers or sure-fire recipes, but you *can* find effective ways to inspire almost every learning style by discovering and appealing to the design of the mind. Remember, it's likely that what motivates *you* will not be as effective with your

211

children. You may have to stretch outside your own perceptions to come up with the right words and methods for your children's unique styles.

Although it is important to understand all the learning styles models, the Gregorc model can best help you to motivate and encourage your children to succeed.[1] Using this model as a foundation, I've asked hundreds of students with various dominant learning styles what really motivates them to do their best, both when it's something they enjoy and when it's something they don't want to do at all. Their answers have been consistent, regardless of age or gender, and you may be surprised at the contrast of their responses. The following comments are representative of the most repeated answers to "What motivates you to do something difficult or boring?"

WHAT MOTIVATES THE DIFFERENT STYLES?

The Dominant Concrete Sequentials—The "Gotta-Have-a-Plan, Just-Say-What-You-Mean, Do-It-by-the-Book" Kids

CSs are nothing if not predictable. They do not like surprises, and they do their best when they know *exactly* what to expect. Their concrete nature makes them practical and hands-on, and their sequential bent keeps them organized and concerned with standards and protocol.

CSs almost always agree that tangible rewards are more motivating than intangible ones. In other words, praise and encouraging words are great, but you need to be specific with your comments (e.g., "I especially like the way you organized your thoughts on paper"), and a job well done should translate to a concrete product (e.g., an award, a grade, money). When it comes to school, CS students claim they are most motivated by knowing that their work will be graded and recorded on permanent school records. Even if an assignment is difficult or boring, you simply need to remind them that it will all count toward the goal at the end, and they'll usually get busy and complete the task.

CSs agree that the way an assignment is first given definitely affects how well they'll complete it. They need clear, specific directions, preferably in writing. The best motivation for them to get started quickly is to see a finished sample that earned the highest grade. CSs also find that being able to break down the assignment into smaller, more manageable parts with distinct and separate deadlines is helpful in giving them continuing proof of accomplishment.

To increase or maintain their level of motivation at home, most CSs agree that it's important to have a checklist written out for their chores and responsibilities. The youngest CSs found it immensely helpful to have a visual chart or checklist, with pictures of what the completed tasks would look like (e.g., a picture of a bed that's made or toys that are put away). Rewards that were motivating ranged from gold stars to small bags of M&Ms or an increase in their allowance.

The CSs also wanted to be clear about what definitely does *not* motivate them. They're quick to point out that they have difficulty dealing with anything vague or general. If you say something like "This house is a mess," it doesn't translate into anything specific enough for CSs to know what you mean. Do you mean you want them to clean it up? What part of it? How soon? What do they get if they do it? Spell out your expectations with as much detail as possible, and the CSs will rarely disappoint you.

The Dominant Abstract Sequentials—The "Let-Me-Think-About-It, Don't-Rush-Me, How-Do-I-Know-This-Is-the-Best-Way" Kids

ASs are dedicated to being as thorough and deliberate as possible in almost everything they do. They usually prefer to take their time, even if it means accepting a penalty for being late.

Since ASs thrive on learning for learning's sake, school does not pose the same motivational problems for them as it does for other students. ASs do not need, and frequently don't want, a lot of frivolous rewards for a job well done. They prefer serious and genuine recognition for their achievements and a higher, more challenging level of work the next time around. They agree that grades are highly motivational, as is the opportunity to excel among their classmates.

At home, ASs will usually participate best when they recognize and appreciate the importance of the goal. They prefer a logical, systematic approach and avoid highly charged, emotional situations. Because of their inherent need to analyze and think through situations, you may have to use more patience in your approach to them, giving them sufficient time to complete each task. When it comes to doing difficult or boring tasks, ASs don't really complain much—they believe they should just do what they have to do and get on with it.

One AS shared that as a teenager, his greatest reward for doing unpleasant chores around the house was his parents' promise of free time when he was finished. Nothing was more precious than having a block of time that was entirely up to him to fill, without the pressure of anyone else's expectations.

ASs are *not* motivated by what they term "cheerleading." They do not appreciate enthusiastic attempts to "pump them up" and get them going. If you try to use any kind of emotional approach, including guilt (e.g., "A child who *really* wanted her mother to be happy would keep her room clean"), you'll usually find ASs unmoved.

The Dominant Abstract Randoms—The "All-for-One-and-One-for-All, Why-Can't-We-All-Just-Get-Along, Let's-Make-Sure-Everyone-Is-Happy" Kids

ARs are not nearly as concerned about facts and details as they are about the *people* involved. Although they're just as smart and capable as any other style, they prefer to not waste their intelligence on anything they don't personally care about or can't apply to their own lives.

ARs are highly motivated by the fact that what they do will please those they most love and respect. At school, most ARs admitted they would work like crazy trying to excel for a teacher who loved them. Since ARs are highly susceptible to guilt, many got high grades because of how it would look to their friends or family if they failed. School is a highly social experience for ARs, so they have to consciously dedicate themselves to completing work that must be done independently. One of the greatest motivations for ARs to get homework assignments done is for them to work together as a group—not necessarily talking to each other about the assignment, but simply being in the same room working toward the same goal.

At home, ARs are often the peacemakers, the buffers between argumentative siblings or frustrated parents. ARs are motivated to do just about anything that will help bring about peace and harmony in the household. The promise of a party, a special event, or a sleep-over at a friend's house is often enough to prompt an AR to do the most difficult or boring task. Anything that can be turned into a social event will hold special appeal.

One mom discovered a unique way to help her AR daughter's study group stay focused on homework without making it seem like such a chore. Once a week, they had a "progressive homework party." Each hour they moved to a different room in the house and had another snack while they studied. Each homework party was scheduled only after the previous one had been deemed a success by the amount and quality of the assignments completed. The ARs actually put pressure on their teachers to give them enough work to last a full evening!

ARs aren't motivated by strict and rigid rules. Although they may obey them out of fear of rejection, they can become silently resentful and the tension may, at some point, lead to a blowup. They don't respond well to someone they perceive is trying to control them. Although you may extract some cooperation by force, ARs will usually find a way to eventually break free.

The Dominant Concrete Randoms—The "Boredom-Is-My-Greatest-Enemy, How-Much-Is-Really-Necessary, I've-Got-a-Great-Idea" Kids

CRs are driven by a need to keep things moving. With quick and usually accurate instincts, CRs rarely spend much time researching or debating options—they just go for it, accepting risks as part of life.

School is often seen as an obstacle for the CRs, a hurdle that must be jumped to finish the race. CRs have a difficult time hiding their boredom, and they rarely have the discipline to sit through a lengthy explanation when they're eager to simply get things over with and move on! If they're absent, CRs are more likely to take a zero on the assignments they missed than to take the time to make up the work. They're rarely motivated to deal with anything that is already in the past; the future is much more appealing. The greatest motivation for excelling in school often comes from working with a teacher who has developed a special relationship with the CR student. CRs agree that they would do the hardest and most boring work in the world if they love and respect the teacher who assigns it.

At home, CRs can often irritate their parents by what appears to be a lack of respect and responsibility. CRs are quick to tell us that it isn't a deliberate move to sabotage the family team; it's just that they don't like to be "bossed around." Most CRs claim they would rather have compelling problems to solve than simply have assigned chores to do.

I recall the story of an exasperated father who got his family together for a conference. "Look," he said, "we've got a problem. None of you wants to do your chores. The house is a mess, the trash isn't getting picked up, the phone messages are getting lost, and there aren't enough clean dishes to get through the next meal. We either have to get our act together or we have to hire a maid." As faces around the table brightened, he added: "If we hire a maid, there'll be a 50 percent cut in allowances, a reduction in groceries, and our vacation to Disneyland is off." Suddenly, his CR recognized a compelling problem. In a matter of minutes, the CR had rallied the troops, and everyone walked away from the table with an assigned task, galvanized by a common goal.

CRs will tell you that they're definitely *not* motivated by rules and requirements. Most CRs don't have trouble with authority; the key is in how the authority is *communicated*. The more you use threats or anger, the more the CR will fail to cooperate with you. Remember, you can't really *make* your child obey. By working with your CR's nature, you'll get greater satisfaction in the end.

HOW DO YOU GET THEM
TO MOTIVATE THEMSELVES?

We as parents need to realize that motivating our children doesn't mean simply getting them to want what *we* want. We first need to determine and define the goal, and then motivate our children to achieve it. Suppose I told you I was going to send you to Antarctica and I was going to give you a multitude of creative ways to get there. If you didn't want to *go* to Antarctica, it wouldn't make any difference how imaginative my methods were—you still wouldn't go.

I have had many frustrated parents assert that their children "have to learn to get along with the world." Sometimes I need to gently remind them that the jails are full of people who didn't *have* to get along with the world. Why not help motivate your children to *want* to get along with the world? Then, if they have a strong and positive relationship with their parents, you'll be the ones they turn to for advice on how to do it.

Sometimes the biggest help parents can be to their growing children is to encourage them to discover for themselves what motivates them. After all, when they leave home, there is usually no one who will try to keep them motivated like you did.

One mom tried the self-motivated approach with her son who simply couldn't seem to remember to take the trash out. She sat down with him and asked, "Andy, what do you think would motivate you to take the trash out on time every week?"

Andy shrugged and said, "Nothing. I don't *want* to take the trash out."

Undaunted, Mom told him she wanted him to think about it and she would ask him again in a couple days. Two days later, she repeated her question. "Andy, have you been thinking about what would motivate you to take out the trash?"

He shrugged again, but said, "Money. Cash money."

"How much money are we talking about?"

"Five thousand dollars," Andy said calmly.

Mom resisted the urge to show her first reaction to this absurd reply. She looked him in the eye and echoed his response. "Five thousand dollars?"

Andy grinned. "Okay, five dollars."

Mom thought a minute. "Okay," she said. "For the next three weeks, I'll give you five dollars if the trash is where it's supposed to be when it's supposed to be there. But after that, I want you to tell me something *else* that will motivate you—something other than money. Maybe a special privilege or some free time."

This approach does two things. First, Andy's mom will not fall into the trap of having to pay for every chore she wants Andy to do. Most important, it gets Andy to think about what *would* motivate him. As he grows up, he needs to learn what it takes to get himself to do things he doesn't want to do. When his mom isn't around to spur him on, he'll know how to inspire himself.

Keep in mind that learning styles, in and of themselves, are value neutral—that is, they're neither bad nor good. There's no single best style, nor does any style make a person smarter or more capable than another. People are so complex that labels never fit neatly anyway. So don't worry about which category your child fits into. If one set of motivation strategies doesn't work, try another.

Sometimes you may simply have to retreat and decide what really needs to be an issue. If you help your child develop worthy goals and ambitions, you'll usually find he/she is much more willing to be motivated to achieve them.

The following chart provides specific ideas for motivating the different learning styles, regardless of their age.

Never Too Late To Motivate!

Dominant Concrete Sequentials
(They need PROOF of accomplishment)

If it's EASY, they'll do it because . . .

- the directions are precise and specific
- the outcome is well-defined and realistically achieved
- there is a definite benefit and a tangible reward

If it's HARD, they'll probably do it if . . .

- you can convince them it will make a difference in their grade
- you can explain the project in a step-by-step manner and/or break down the assignment into smaller parts
- you can provide some examples of successful work

Dominant Abstract Sequentials
(They need a SENSE of accomplishment)

If it's EASY, they'll do it because . . .

- it's logical and makes sense
- the goal is well-defined and worthwhile
- it contributes to a general love of learning

If it's HARD, they'll probably do it if . . .

- it comes from a credible source and appears to be reliable
- they are given enough time and advance notice
- they can see where it fits into the greater scheme of things

Never Too Late To Motivate!

Dominant Abstract Randoms
(They need a FEELING of accomplishment)

If it's EASY, they'll do it because . . .

- everyone they like or admire is doing it, too

- it's fun and provides variety and flexibility

- the teacher is someone they really like

If it's HARD, they'll probably do it if . . .

- it will help them feel loved and accepted by parents and peers

- you can convince them it will personally affect their lives for the better

- it's really important to someone they love

Dominant Concrete Randoms
(They need the REWARDS of accomplishment)

If it's EASY, they'll do it because . . .

- there's a sense of adventure—something to be conquered

- it's compelling, fast-moving, and intriguing

- they can treat it lightheartedly and with a sense of humor

If it's HARD, they'll probably do it if . . .

- they are convinced it can get them where they want to go

- they are doing it for someone who really loves and appreciates them

- they can hit the high points and then move on

Plan of Action

Fill out a separate sheet of paper for each child, and answer the following questions:

1. What is_____(child's name) most motivated by?
2. What is_____least motivated by?

Now ask each child (providing he/she is old enough) to answer the same questions. Compare your answers and discuss.

Chapter Five

Turning Conflict into Cooperation

"It's not my *turn* to clean up the kitchen!"
"Mom, make him stop *looking* at me like that!"
"But Dad said I *could!*"
"She *always* gets the best jobs!"

Do any of these statements sound familiar? If your household is not as peaceful and harmonious as you'd like it to be, maybe everyone at home could use a little practice in appreciating each other's learning style strengths. It's ironic that we seem to be drawn to people who possess the traits and characteristics that we lack. When I married my husband, who is totally opposite from me in style, I thought I was simply getting a refreshingly different perspective. I quickly realized it wasn't so refreshing when I had to translate much of what I said into a language his learning style could understand. Working through our differences has helped us realize that the strengths each of us brought to the relationship could combine to make us a strong team.

However, just about the time we began to get a handle on how each of *us* processed information, along came our two sons, each bringing with him a whole new set of communication challenges!

In this chapter, I'd like to give you some ideas on how to turn family conflict into cooperation. First we're going to look at the strengths each dominant learning style can bring to the family when we focus on the positive aspects of individual differences. Then, armed with this knowledge, we'll see how we can apply what we've learned to smooth potential trouble spots in our family relationships. Remember, none of us possesses a pure learning style, but we can all admit to having definite bents and patterns of learning.

WHAT EACH STYLE CAN CONTRIBUTE TO THE FAMILY

Auditory

You can spot the auditory learners by their need to talk. Their strength lies in their ability to work through a thought process verbally, using trusted friends or family members as sounding boards. You don't usually have to wonder what an auditory person is thinking—just listen and you'll know!

Visual

The visual learners are good at capturing a verbal concept by using a vivid picture or chart. If you're having a hard time imagining how something will look, often the visual family member can bring the idea to life on paper for you.

Kinesthetic

These learners have a high degree of energy, which can be a plus when you've run out of steam. Take advantage of the restless and animated spirit of the kinesthetic family member by letting him/her run the errands, chase the dreams, and keep everyone moving.

Analytic

Analytics can look at the big picture and break it down into manageable parts. Their natural ability to bring order out of chaos can be invaluable. In overwhelming situations when you aren't sure where to begin, the analytic family member can help you identify a good starting point.

Globals

Globals are better than most at grasping an overall concept and then translating it into terms almost everyone can understand. They're also great at figuring out how small pieces fit into a big picture.

Concrete Sequentials

CSs are strong in organization and detail, and they can quickly figure out how much time a project will actually take. Another of their gifts is the ability to take someone's great idea and turn it into a practical, concrete product.

Abstract Sequentials

ASs can be a wonderful resource for checking and documenting information. ASs will take the time and effort to research and evaluate information and make sure that the facts are right, the values are genuine, and the sources are credible.

Abstract Randoms

ARs have an intuitive sense of others' needs and feelings, and they are gifted peacemakers. They often provide the glue that keeps the family together, constantly searching for ways to keep everyone happy. ARs will also provide spontaneity and flexibility, even in the most difficult circumstances.

Concrete Randoms

CRs will always keep things interesting. They are visionaries who dare to dream the impossible. They can inspire, motivate, and energize the rest of the family. The CR family member will make sure no one stagnates or loses momentum, constantly pushing the envelope toward new adventures.

HOW UNDERSTANDING EACH STYLE
CAN REDUCE FAMILY CONFLICT

Acknowledging the individual learning styles within your family is the first step toward bringing everyone together as a team. The next step is *understanding* how these various styles manifest themselves, because only then will you be able to depersonalize conflict every time it crops up.

During a recent seminar series, a grateful mom told me how understanding learning styles had brought her family closer together. Her husband is a career military officer and a dominant Concrete Sequential. His strict and rigid approach to dealing with his dominantly Concrete Random, global teenage daughter, Amy, created almost unbearable friction between them. Then Amy took a two-week learning styles course through her school and began eagerly relating her experiences to her parents. Their curiosity piqued, Mom and Dad attended one of my seminar series to see what the concept was all about. Shortly after, Dad came home one evening to find that Amy had not completed the tasks he'd left for her. As he launched into a stern and detailed lecture, Amy interrupted him. "Oh, Dad—you're being so *CS!*" To Mom's amazement, Dad began to smile, and soon both he and Amy were laughing. With the tension broken, father and daughter began to negotiate deadlines for the assigned tasks.

Often just referring to what you need in less personal terms can make a big difference in how you and your children relate to, and cooperate with, each other. Saying "I need you to be real sequential for a few minutes" sounds a lot nicer than "Do you think you could *focus* for a few minutes?" The bottom-line accountability doesn't need to change at all—just the method for helping your children achieve it.

WHEN PARENTS HAVE DIFFERENT LEARNING STYLES

Chances are good that in every family where there are two parents, there will be two different learning styles. Although the potential for great teamwork exists, there's also room for conflict between parenting styles. The analytic parent may emphasize the importance of maintaining a consistent code of conduct, while the global parent insists there needs to be room for exceptions. The sequential parent may dictate a predictable routine, while the random counterpart has difficulty even remembering what the routine is supposed to *be.* Since these parents probably have children with different learning styles, how can they present a unified front? How can they agree on parenting strategies for their children when they may not even agree on what's most important between the two of them?

Parents of opposite styles must make a concentrated effort not to work against each other's style. Identify the outcomes and goals you want to set for your family before you discuss the methods you think are needed for achieving them. Once you have agreed on those bottom-line outcomes, recognize that each of you may have different approaches. As long as you're both committed to the objective, give yourselves room for compromise. As soon as your children are old enough, enlist their help in establishing basic family policies. Then talk about some of the various ways to reach the same destination, emphasizing the importance of the bottom line.

If you're a single parent, it's even more critical for your children to recognize and appreciate learning style differences. When your children realize that you're not *deliberately* trying to frustrate and annoy them, they may also understand that the way they're using their styles is making life more difficult for you. Though all of you may become exhausted in your efforts to make the team work, you'll find that your energies are well rewarded when you recognize how valuable you are to each other.

FOCUSING ON THE BEST

The following charts provide examples of how you can make the most of individual family learning style strengths while working toward a common goal during two stressful times of the year: the holidays and summer. Remember, cooperation means that everyone recognizes and appreciates each other's *strengths*, focusing on the *best* aspects of each person.

Peace on Earth at Home During the Holidays

Don't let the holiday season provide more stress than it does happiness. This year, try to make the most of the gifts God created in each individual. Remember that each family member is unique, and sometimes the best gift of all is understanding.

For Dominant Concrete Sequentials

Quick Review of What They Need:

> *Organization*
> *Predictability*
> *Scheduled routine*
> *Literal communication*
> *Contingency plans (What if?)*
> *A beginning, a middle, and an end*
> *Step-by-step instructions*
> *Tangible rewards*

- Put them in charge of recording everyone's wish list for Christmas gifts. They can help design a form that can be filled out, or they can simply record each person's list on a sheet of paper.
- Let them be in charge of organizing, sorting, and arranging the gifts under the tree. Encourage them to check for loose gift tags or torn paper. When it's time to open the gifts, put them in charge of distribution.
- Give them the ads in the weekend newspaper, and let them find items and/or coupons for the things that appear on each family member's wish list. Provide an envelope for each person's list for appropriate coupons and ads.

For Dominant Abstract Sequentials

Quick Review of What They Need:

    Lots of time to work through a project
    Resource material
    Logical, step-by-step instruction
    Credible sources of information
    Opportunities for analysis
    Appreciation for their ideas and advice

- Put them in charge of finding the best price for items on the family's wish lists. Help them comparison shop through the newspaper ads or through the envelopes that the Concrete Sequential sibling provides.
- Challenge them to figure out how much money it would take to buy everything that everybody wants on his/her list for Christmas.
- Let them come up with some ideas for gift giving for an adopt-a-child or adopt-a-family project. Help them decide which gifts make the most sense, given the parameters (age, needs, etc.).

For Dominant Abstract Randoms

Quick Review of What They Need:

    A personal reason for doing almost anything
    Frequent praise and reassurance of worth
    Acceptance and appreciation of personal feelings and "illogical"
        opinions
    An opportunity to work with someone else
    A feeling of harmony with virtually everyone
    An opportunity to use creativity and imagination

- Challenge them to help the house look and feel like the real spirit of Christmas. What kind of decorations will we need? How many can we make ourselves?

- Let them select names from the adopt-a-family gift tree and help decide what to buy. Besides the actual gifts for the adopted family, what could we make ourselves that would communicate Christmas love?
- Let them decide how they would like to present the Christmas story before the family celebrates by opening gifts.

For Dominant Concrete Randoms

Quick Review of What They Need:
> *Inspiration*
> *Compelling reasons*
> *Independence*
> *Freedom to choose*
> *Opportunities to provide alternatives*
> *Guidelines instead of rules*

- Challenge them to come up with a new annual family tradition for Christmas. Be specific and firm with parameters (how much it could cost, who it would involve, etc.).
- Let them propose a holiday family outing during Christmas vacation. Give them a budget and guidelines, and challenge them to find the best place to go. (Give them extra credit if they can find coupons or discounts!)
- Encourage them to participate on their own as well as with the family in an adopt-a-child program. Offer to match whatever money they can provide for a gift, and challenge them to "shop till you drop."

For the Kinesthetic, Highly Active Child

Remember: The chances are good that you may not be a kinesthetic, highly active person yourself, so try to understand the need for constant motion.

For younger children: Keep them moving! How about running "errands" such as checking the Christmas lights and reporting which ones are out, or having at least one meal a day that's a "movable feast" (eat each course in a different location).

For older children: Keep them moving! When they come to the store with you, give them a clipboard and a checklist of items to be found in the store. Have them write down the location and price of each item. Maybe have a "mystery item" that you list only by description and price; if they find it, they win a small prize or an extra privilege.

Summer Survival Sheet

"I'm bored—there's nothing to do!"
"This is dumb—why did we have to come here?"
"Mom! She hit me!"
"Make him stop looking at me!"
"Why do we always have to go camping together?"

It's summer, and school's out. Now you get to spend more time with your children. Uh-oh, let's admit it—sometimes spending more time as a family sparks conflict and strife along with the desired togetherness. If you hear any of the above statements coming from *your* children, here are some ideas to help you survive.

For Dominant Concrete Sequentials

(the gotta-have-a-plan, just-say-what-you-mean,
do-it-by-the-book kids)

- Put them in charge of the calendar. Buy or make an oversized calendar of the summer months and post it on the kitchen wall. Fill in all the events and activities you have planned, and be sure to designate certain dates as unplanned, spontaneous fun days.
- For the major trips or summer events, let these kids design a checklist for items that will be needed. Encourage them to talk to each family member about what he/she will need and compile individual as well as group checklists to be completed before the trip.
- Ask them to design at least one contingency plan for each major summer event. For example, what happens if it rains and you can't do the outdoor picnic for the family reunion?

For the Dominant Abstract Sequentials

*(the let-me-think-about-it, don't-rush-me,
how-do-I-know-this-is-the-best-way kids)*

- Put them in charge of finding the best price for the items on the checklist made by the Concrete Sequentials for the family trip. Help them comparison shop through newspaper ads or garage sales.
- Challenge them to figure out a family vacation budget for the summer, taking into account major and minor trips and events.
- Prepare them for changes in the calendar with as much advance notice as possible, even if it's only a few minutes. For example, as all of you are getting ready to go roller-skating, don't say, "Hey! I've got a great idea! Let's go swimming instead of skating!" Instead, say, "Hey, what would you think about going swimming instead of skating?" Then let them think about or even briefly discuss the pros and cons for a few minutes before coming to a decision.

For the Dominant Abstract Randoms

*(the all-for-one-one-for-all, why-can't-we-all-just-get-along,
let's-make-everyone-happy kids)*

- Let them be the "social chairperson." Commission them to find out what would make each family member happy. Armed with the calendar and checklists made by siblings, let them interview family members and add a personal touch to each person's checklist.
- Let them plan for the times when having friends over along with the family would be appropriate. Help them distinguish between family times and party times, and give them a lot of input into the party times.
- Let them write in a few days over the summer that are "do-nothing days." These are days when they can actually do absolutely nothing if they feel like it and do so guilt-free.

For the Dominant Concrete Randoms

*(the boredom-is-my-greatest-enemy,
let's-keep-things-moving, I've-got-a-great-idea kids)*

- Challenge them to come up with new adventures for family outings this summer. Be specific and firm with your parameters (cost, distance, etc.) and then let them use their imagination.
- Encourage them to design ways to earn or save money during the summer, especially those kids who are too young to get a formal job. Again, be specific and firm with your parameters, but challenge them to think about ways to make money and cut costs. (For example, give them a percentage of each coupon they find that you actually use.)
- Offer incentives for cooperation during family gatherings and events. For example, if they go on a family event without complaining, they can host their own summer party or outing for a few of their friends.

Don't let the lazy, crazy days of summer provide more stress than happiness. This year, try to make the most of the gifts God created in each individual in your family, and remember to discover and appreciate the way they learn!

Plan of Action

What is your greatest challenge for working together as a family? Try holding a family meeting and deciding on one project you would like to accomplish together. Be sure everyone gives input, and try to assign individual responsibilities that will match each person's learning style strengths.

Chapter Six

Dealing
with Issues of
Discipline

She looked like such an adorable, little girl. "Angela!" Her mother sounded exasperated. "Angela, I said get over here *right this minute!*"

I watched the face of this beautiful five-year-old standing in the aisle of the department store suddenly darken with a scowl.

"*No!*" she cried. "I want to go see the toys *now!*"

Her mother looked exhausted as she grabbed Angela's hand and began to drag her, screaming, through the store. As they passed me, I saw the mother's eyes roll upward as she muttered, "Just another ordinary day."

If you're the parent of a strong-willed child, you know how frustrating it can be to see your bright, loving, creative offspring turn suddenly into a stubborn, immovable force. What did you do to deserve such defiance? How can this wonderful kid turn into such a monster?

Frustrated parents all over the world face the challenge of disciplining their children without breaking their spirit. As loving parents, we want to do what's best, but it's often difficult for us to accept and remember that each child is different and unique and responds to some forms of discipline better than others. Though this brings a distinct challenge to the concept and practice of effective discipline, it also assures us that we can maintain bottom-line accountability while we honor each child's style.

Before I outline specific discipline strategies for dealing with each learning style, let me remind you of some essential concepts that can be effective with *all* styles.

ESSENTIAL STRATEGIES FOR ALL LEARNING STYLES

1. Authority and accountability should always stay intact. I was one of those Concrete Random, strong-willed kids, and I can tell you that virtually every child wants to respect authority and expects to be held accountable. An understanding of learning style strengths can actually help you reinforce accountability by communicating your authority in a way that makes the most sense to each child.

2. Remember, you can't force your child to obey. When I became a new mother of twins, I made a startling and frustrating discovery. Although these babies were less than seven pounds each, there were still certain things I simply could not *force* them to do! For example, I couldn't force them to love me or respect me. Like it or not, each of us, no matter how young, has a free will. As parents, we must realize that we cannot force our children to obey simply because we demand that they do.

3. The strength and quality of your relationship with your child has more power than any discipline technique. This concept is closely related to the preceding one. Since we can't force our children to obey us, the better our relationship with them, the more likely they are to respond positively to our guidance. Early in my parenting career, I made a profound discovery regarding my strong-willed child Michael. During the times that he and I aren't "locking horns," I work hard at maintaining a solid and loving relationship with him. As a result, he and I are close. When I am upset with him, he can't stand to have our relationship on such poor terms. As a result, my disciplinary efforts are more effective. If your children don't care that you're upset with them, your efforts at disciplining them will have little impact. If you do have a good, loving relationship with your children, nurture it by exercising your disciplinary power carefully. Children are particularly sensitive to heavy-handedness and injustice, which can cause a good relationship to quickly sour.

4. *Remember to ask yourself, "What's the point?"* Even young children need to know *why* things are important. Our children don't have to *agree* with our reasons, but we do owe them the courtesy of an explanation if they want one. If you find yourself arguing frequently with your child and it has turned into a power struggle, try calmly stating the reason for what you're asking, and then state the consequences for disobedience. If your child continues to disobey, follow through with the consequences. Remember, the action you take will be much more effective than the anger or other emotions you show. If you raise your voice often when disciplining your child, insisting that he/she had better do what you say or else, you may find that you've been tuned out.

With older kids, let them have some input into the situation. Define your parameters and be specific about your goals. Then ask for their ideas when it comes to accomplishing the goals. Be firm and friendly when letting everyone know up front what the consequences for disobedience will be, and make sure you reinforce the entire conversation with love and appreciation for their participation in the process.

ESSENTIAL STRATEGIES FOR INDIVIDUAL LEARNING STYLES

The key to successfully communicating authority and meting out discipline usually lies in *how* you do it. The following strategies can help you accomplish important goals with your children without sacrificing accountability, but also without squelching the natural design of their minds.

For Highly Kinesthetic Children

For these kids, put as much action into your words as possible. With younger children, for example, you may need to actually pick them up and physically remove them from a room. Use bodily movements as much as you can to illustrate what you're saying (e.g., sign language or hand motions). Sometimes you may be able to literally "walk them through" a particular situation.

One exasperated mother had told her active five-year-old son numerous times *not* to rub the cat's fur the wrong way. When the perturbed feline showed up with its hair again standing on end, the mom had had enough. She took her son's hand, held it under her own, and gently but firmly smoothed the cat's fur. After a few seconds of maintaining the rhythm, she removed her hand and was delighted to see her son continue stroking the cat's fur properly.

For Highly Auditory Children

When you lay out rules or discuss consequences, ask your highly auditory child to repeat what you said. Remember that auditory learners often remember best what they can put into a rhyme or song. Since having a sense of humor usually helps immensely, try coming up with some "consequence rhymes"—for example, "Not in time, end of the line!" or "Jump from the chair, nothing new to wear!"

For Highly Visual Children

Often something as simple as a poster or illustrated checklist is enough to drive home a point to your visual child. When I was a child, my parents had a plaque with a doghouse and four removable wooden dogs bearing the names of each family member hanging on hooks outside the doghouse. Whenever any of us (Mom and Dad included) got in trouble for some reason, the dog bearing our name was placed inside the doghouse. To this day, the visual impact of being "in the doghouse" has had a lasting effect!

For Dominantly Analytic Learners

Be as specific as possible when you're disciplining your analytic child or teenager. Dealing with a general situation is too overwhelming—break it down into smaller, more manageable parts. For example, when dealing with the issue of broken curfew, instead of saying "We can't have you breaking curfew, Tom!" say something like "Tom, we need you to be home on weeknights no later than 10:00 P.M. Last night you didn't get in until 10:30."

With your analytic child or teenager, it's important to separate the deed from the doer. The less personal you can make your criticism, the better—for example, "Susan, you must have done this without thinking. I know this doesn't make you look as smart as you are." (Please note that this will *not* work with the more global children—they almost always take *everything* personally!)

For Dominantly Global Learners

For kids with this learning style, always start with an overall statement of love and support before you focus specifically on any wrongdoing. These children need to maintain a general sense of well-being, knowing your love is unconditional and not dependent upon their behavior. For example, "John, I've never loved anyone more than I love you, and it really disappoints me that this happened." Often it's best not to recount specific details of the offense unless you honestly believe your child doesn't understand what he/she did wrong. A more general statement may suffice: "Do you understand why you're in trouble?"

If you yourself are more analytic, it may be difficult to remember how important it is to your global children that you don't immediately tell them exactly what behavior needs to be changed. For globals, the indirect approach is almost always more effective than the frontal attack. For example, instead of saying "Allison, you need to take that trash out right now," you may get a better response from a hint: "Boy, that trash is really beginning to smell bad!" Suddenly, Allison pipes up, "Oh yeah, I've got to take it out now."

For Dominant Concrete Sequentials

For most CSs, when it comes to discipline, consistency goes a long way. Establish certain unchanging rules, and write them down. For the visual CSs, suggest they find pictures to illustrate each rule. Make sure the CSs know what the consequences for disobedience will be, and be sure to follow through in each situation. If you're a dominantly random parent, your best bet will be choosing as few and as simple rules as possible so you won't forget or be tempted to suddenly change your mind.

Help your CSs cope with exceptions to the rules by giving as much notice as possible. For example, "Kelli, I know we don't usually let you stay up after 10:00 P.M., but tomorrow we're going to need to bend that rule a little."

For Dominant Abstract Sequentials

For AR children, justice is an important concept. What's fair for one is fair for all. A dominantly random parent runs the greatest risk of being viewed as weak or inconsistent simply by virtue of wanting to consider mitigating circumstances. Be clear in your expectations and logical in your punishments and consequences. Be sure your AS understands the purpose for a particular rule, and whenever possible, try to allow the AS to have at least some input into the setting of rules in the first place.

Although it's always important to show children how much we love them, too much emotion is often difficult for AS children to handle. For example, the more you are visibly upset or angry, the more likely it will be that your AS will be less responsive and may withdraw completely.

For Dominant Abstract Randoms

For most ARs, the whole process of discipline, criticism, or correction is traumatic. Because harmony is so important, ARs will often need less discipline simply because they try so hard to please their parents and keep peace in the family. When it's necessary to punish your AR child, always surround every word or action with love. You can do this sincerely while still driving home the point. For example, "Sandy, you're very important to me. I can't let you behave like this. Will you help me keep our relationship on good terms?"

Because ARs are so susceptible to guilt, you should make a conscious effort to use it sparingly. Your aim should not be to make ARs feel bad—that will happen automatically. The purpose in your punishment should be to correct a problem and reassure your AR that your love and acceptance remain unchanged.

For Dominant Concrete Randoms

CRs may present the greatest challenge when it comes to discipline. You'll find that traditional methods of punishment often will not work with them. CRs believe that, for the most part, rules are simply *guidelines*, meant to be followed to the letter only if absolutely necessary. If you're a CS parent, you may find yourself frequently confronting your CR child over specific issues in which the CR claims he/she essentially did what you wanted but just didn't do it the *way* you wanted it done. With CRs, it's especially important to answer the question "What's the point?" You'll have greater success in maintaining discipline if you can be more flexible with the methods than with the bottom-line accountability.

Most CRs do not have trouble with authority—they have trouble with how that authority is *communicated*. The best way to explain it is what I call my *drive-through theory*. When I stop at a fast-food drive-through and give my order to the little box, I often hear something like "That will be $3.86. Please drive forward." Isn't that a keen sense of the obvious? Give me a break! Do they think I'm too stupid to know I'm supposed to go to the window? By the time I get up to the cashier, I'm so irritated I never want to come back. On the other hand, when I hear "That will be $3.86 at the first window, please," I know exactly what I'm supposed to pay and exactly where I'm supposed to go. But it's said in a way that assumes I'm a smart and capable person. Now that may not seem like a big deal to a lot of people, but to us CRs, it's essential that we're given a little credit for knowing the right thing to do.

NO QUICK RECIPES

Always remember that each child is a complex and wonderful mixture of learning style strengths—and that there's a little bit of all styles in every one of us! When it's necessary to discipline a child, it's usually stressful at best. Don't worry about memorizing specific techniques or labels. Use some variety and flexibility in your strategies, constantly monitoring and adjusting to find what really works.

You may not have to apologize to your children for the outcomes you expect, but you may occasionally need to say you're sorry for forcing them to use only your methods for achieving them.

There is one more important point I'd like to make. Every parent knows there are times when you simply can't negotiate, days when you're too exhausted to strike a bargain, situations that have made you too frustrated to figure out a strategy that will work with your child's learning style. If you're making an honest effort most of the time to use the ideas and strategies that work with each individual child's learning strengths, you'll find that in situations in which you need to just "pull rank" and insist your children obey you because you're the parent and you *said* so, they will be surprisingly more cooperative. If you use this approach sparingly, you'll find it has the power and influence necessary to keep your children responsive to your authority.

The following charts will give you a little more practice in developing a variety of strategies for reaching accountability using the unique design of each child's mind. Even when the discipline dilemma is universal and ageless, you may be surprised to discover how many different reasons there are for bad behaviors and how many effective tactics you can use for solving the problems.

Universal Discipline Problem: Bedtime Battles

Reasons Why   *Things to Try*

Dominant Concrete Sequentials

1. There is no predictability about night-time routines.

2. A change in schedule comes about too abruptly.

3. There are still too many things that need to be done.

1. Establish a bedtime routine and stick to it; post it visually, if it helps.

2. Give at least a two-minute warning before bedtime so they can prepare themselves.

3. At least 30 minutes before bedtime, check with them to see what still needs to be done and how you can help.

Dominant Abstract Sequentials

1. Tasks started are not yet completed.

2. They are not prepared for the next day.

3. There is no sense of closure to the day.

1. Help them prepare early, completing tasks and events to their satisfaction.

2. Arrange clothes and materials for the next day.

3. At least one hour before bedtime, check to see what they feel must be done before bed, and see what you can do to help.

Dominant Abstract Randoms

1. They don't want to disconnect from friends and family.

2. They feel too isolated alone in the bed-room.

3. They don't feel there is anything to look forward to tomorrow.

1. Ask them what will comfort them most—a stuffed animal, a night light, leaving the door open?

2. Establish a personal, close night-time routine—reading a book, a quiet conver-sation, prayers, etc.

3. Spend a few moments talking about the next day, not from a preparation stand-point but in a way that builds enthusiasm and anticipation.

Reasons Why   *Things to Try*

Dominant Concrete Randoms

Reasons Why	Things to Try
1. They feel a lack of control.	1. Allow some negotiation on minor points—which bed, what pajamas, which night light, etc.
2. Their energy level is still high.	2. Be sure they have had lots of opportunities to burn up energy well before bedtime, even if you have to make up excuses for running errands, etc.
3. They have too many things on their minds.	3. Help them talk through what happened today (but don't press for details!), and talk about what will happen tomorrow.

Universal Discipline Problem: Lack of Respect

Reasons Why   *Things to Try*

Dominant Concrete Sequentials

1. The random parent seems inconsistent or unreliable.

2. They are frustrated because they don't know what's expected of them.

3. They believe everyone should do things their way.

---

1. Establish simple, bottom-line rules you can consistently enforce; be clear about "truth and consequences."

2. Keep them focused on what you need to have them accomplish; be as specific as possible.

3. Point out how many ways there may be to achieve any one goal.

Dominant Abstract Sequentials

1. The parent isn't as systematic and logical as they are.

2. They become impatient with the parent who lacks structure.

3. Their preference to be alone makes them seem aloof or distant.

---

1. State bottom-line accountability and calmly lay out the consequences. Ask "Do you think that's fair?" If they say it's not, press for their reasoning and logically work through the issue.

2. Try to schedule times to explain and discuss expectations. Give them the opportunity for input and limited debate.

3. Try not to take the aloofness personally; give them some time and distance to respond to you.

Reasons Why   *Things to Try*

Dominant Abstract Randoms

---

1. They are defensive and feel inadequate because they lack strong sequential ordering ability.

2. They succumb to peer pressure—it just seems like the thing to do.

3. They resist what they see as your constant efforts to change "who they are."

1. Be sure they understand that your discipline doesn't affect your love for them.

2. Don't force them to choose between their peers and you—encourage them to see how their actions can influence their friends.

3. Recognize that there may be many ways to achieve a goal—be as flexible as possible right up to the bottom line.

Dominant Concrete Randoms

---

1. They sense a lack of respect from you in the way that you treat them.

2. They resist doing something just because you said so.

3. They are constantly looking for short cuts and opportunities for negotiation.

1. Don't state the obvious—assume they are intelligent and capable; acknowledge their uniqueness, and enforce the bottom line.

2. Avoid ultimatums and statements beginning with "You must," "You will," "There's no way you're going to . . . "

3. Make the distinction clear between negotiable and nonnegotiable issues; be as flexible as possible.

Plan of Action

Fill out a separate sheet of paper for each of your children. At the top, write down an issue that has often become a discipline problem between you and this child. Divide the paper into two columns; label one side "Reasons Why," and the other, "Things to Try." Then start writing as many things as you can think of in both columns. If your child is old enough, discuss what you've written and ask if he/she agrees with you.

Chapter Seven

What's the Big Deal About School?

Many students are much more intelligent than school has shown them to be. Likewise, many parents have been convinced that there is something wrong with their children when that simply may not be true. Traditional classrooms, inflexible systems of measurement and evaluation, and established methods of instruction don't fit every student. You know your child is bright and capable; you understand that children need to learn discipline and structure, but what happens when your child seems to constantly be at odds with the school system? Do you automatically assume your child is doing something wrong?

Our children spend a significant part of their lives going to school, and their self-esteem reflects, to a great degree, how well they're perceived by educators on their "permanent records." But how much of school should really be such a big deal? How can parents know when their children really lack basic skills as opposed to when their children simply don't fit into a standard mold?

Obviously, there are no simple answers, but I would challenge you to take a serious look at the many different ways of being intelligent. If you can help your children identify their learning style strengths, you can also point out why those same strengths can become obstacles when they encounter various academic demands in the classroom. Let's look at some of these demands in light of what's hardest for each of the dominant learning styles.

WHAT'S HARDEST FOR EACH LEARNING STYLE?

Auditory Learners

Difficulty 1: Not talking in class. Because of the need to verbalize their thought processes, auditory learners often don't even realize they're talking. As soon as the teacher says something that "clicks," they quickly turn to someone and talk about it. Since using other students as sounding boards is often frowned upon in traditional classrooms, the auditory learner finds comments on his/her report card such as "Needs to practice listening skills" or "Has trouble paying attention during class."

How to Help: Try talking through the issue of finding appropriate times to speak up at school. You may need to actually help your auditory children practice being quiet or verbalizing ideas to themselves before talking to someone else.

Difficulty 2: Reading silently. In order to remember what they're reading, most auditory learners prefer to read aloud. Even when they're forced to read silently, they may read more slowly simply because they're still verbalizing each and every word to themselves. Any other sounds that are made in the room while auditory students are trying to read may be even more amplified and distracting because they're already trying to listen to the sound of their own voices.

How to Help: Don't put a lot of pressure on your auditory children to read more rapidly as long as they demonstrate an adequate level of comprehension and recall. Point out how important the verbalizing is for understanding and remembering the information, realizing that sometimes this means auditory students will need to move their lips when they read.

Difficulty 3: Blurting out the answer instead of raising their hands. Since auditory learners tend to think out loud, it's difficult to stop thoughts from overflowing into speech. Often auditory students don't even realize they're talking until they're already in trouble for doing it.

How to Help: Again, helping your auditory children become aware of why this is happening and then actually practicing situations in which it can be avoided will help more than you may think.

Visual Learners

Difficulty 1: Listening to a lecture without visual aids. Despite their best efforts, most visual learners will quickly lose their concentration if they have nothing to focus on visually. At that point, just about everything becomes a distraction—posters on the wall, people walking outside in the hall, and so on. Teachers may notice these students develop a faraway look, drifting into inattention or creating a distraction among their classmates.

How to Help: Make your visual learners aware of how important it is to have something that helps them focus their imagination while listening. If the teacher does not provide what they need, help students develop coping strategies. For example, they can try drawing a picture or diagram of what the teacher is talking about, then add lines or shapes as the idea develops.

Difficulty 2: Being restricted to white paper or standard blue or black ink. Because visual people thrive on stimulating colors and textures, it's frustrating for them to confine their creativity to sterile white paper or boring colors of ink. Some teachers may become impatient with the lack of uniformity on assignment papers, thus insisting that all students be consistent.

How to Help: It often helps to let the visual child use colorful folders, envelopes, and notebooks, especially when the papers inside can't look as creative. Make a point of letting your children choose their own school materials whenever possible.

Kinesthetic Learners

Difficulty 1: Sitting still. No one fidgets and squirms better than the highly kinesthetic child! Everything from constantly changing position in the chair to actually getting up several times to walk around or go to the bathroom seems to be a normal part of a kinesthetic's day. These children can certainly drive their teachers crazy simply by maintaining an unceasing flow of energy and movement. Even when a kinesthetic child is sitting at his/her desk, some part of his/her body is usually still moving—toes tapping, head bobbing, eyes darting around the room.

How to Help: If your kinesthetic child has a teacher who is not willing to let him/her keep moving while listening or working, you'll need to teach your child coping techniques. Sometimes doodling while listening helps the child to focus. Using a highlighter to keep track of the material the teacher is talking about is also a great help. (This may mean buying a copy of the textbook for your child so he/she can write in it.) A worry stone or squishy ball will also help a child quietly squeeze out some energy without causing any trouble in class.

Difficulty 2: Doing the same thing for longer than 10 minutes at a time. Even if kinesthetic children manage to sit still and concentrate on a task, it's unrealistic to expect uninterrupted attention for more than a few minutes. The more you can keep them moving, the greater their concentration. Unfortunately, a teacher often judges how well students are listening by how quiet and still they are.

How to Help: Some teachers have agreed to let their kinesthetic pupils have more than one assigned seat. As long as they're in one seat or the other and can prove they're listening, they're not required to sit in the same place for long periods of time. If it's not possible for your child to move much at school, at least design homework and study time at home to be as flexible and movable as possible.

Difficulty 3: Looking at you when you talk to them. Robert is my highly kinesthetic son. Although he has an excellent memory and is quick to remember large chunks of data, he can't recount the Pledge of Allegiance if I make him stand still and look at me. When I let him pace, wander, and recite, he almost never makes a mistake. If I insist that he stop and focus on me, his mind quickly goes blank.

How to Help: If your kinesthetic child is getting in trouble because he/she won't look the teacher in the eye, encourage the teacher to hold the child accountable for the information, whether or not the student is standing still. If the teacher refuses to cooperate, do your best to explain to your child why it's so difficult to concentrate without moving and that it's not a reflection of intelligence.

Analytic Learners

Difficulty 1: Identifying the main idea. When they're reading or listening, analytic learners naturally pick up details. While they're busy focusing on the specifics, however, the general concept may elude them altogether. This may account for situations in which a teacher *knows* those students read the material carefully, but they just didn't *get* it.

How to Help: Because analytic learners have difficulty pulling the general from the specific, they often have trouble studying for tests. Before your child sits down to read material he/she is going to be tested on, quickly suggest two or three possibilities for the main idea. This can serve as a gentle reminder that there is an overall purpose for reading the selection.

Difficulty 2: Summarizing or paraphrasing. Since analytics are naturally prone to remember details more than trying to get a general sense of why the details are significant, asking them to put something "in a nutshell" can be extremely difficult. Questions like "What do you think this means?" can be met with perplexed stares from the analytic who is trying to figure out what in the world you're talking about.

How to Help: One of the best methods for helping analytics put a passage into their own words is to encourage them to read with a highlighter. Help them learn to highlight key words, then go back and write a summary using those words. The more they do this, the easier it will become to automatically read with the idea that summarizing will be necessary when they finish.

Difficulty 3: Answering essay questions. Many analytic students quickly and efficiently tackle the essay questions on an exam only to get the scored test back with comments like "You need to expand your ideas" or "Try giving more examples." Analytics are good at outlining and concisely stating information. However, if the teacher asking for that information happens to be more global, the answers may seem too short, the supporting statements too abbreviated.

How to Help: Encourage your analytic student to clarify what the teacher is asking for on an essay test. How many examples should be given? What kind of answer is considered too short? If the teacher will not give an answer that satisfies the analytic, try helping your child design a formula for answering every essay question. For example: (1) state your purpose; (2) give at least two reasons; and (3) write a conclusion.

Global Learners

Difficulty 1: Outlining material. Most globals struggle with the process of outlining because their minds naturally jump ahead before all the details can be covered. Since they're most concerned with getting the overall idea down, the details often show up too late, and the outline must be rewritten. Trying to write an outline of a research project or speech without knowing what the final outcome will be is almost impossible for them. Many a global has burned the midnight oil trying to write an entire paper so the preliminary outline could be handed in on time.

How to Help: One of the most effective methods for helping globals produce a formal outline is what many call "webbing" or "mapping." Start with a clean piece of paper and write the main idea in the middle. Then, in no particular order, begin to write down everything that branches out from the main idea, like limbs from the trunk of a tree. As each idea comes to mind, draw another line below the concept it should be attached to, and keep filling the page. At the end, pull out another clean sheet of paper and begin transferring the information from the web to a formal outline. You'll be amazed at how analytic the product will look!

Difficulty 2: Remembering details without knowing what to listen for in the first place. One of the scariest sentences globals can hear in school is: "Now, I'm going to read these instructions to you only once." Their minds begin to race ahead, trying to figure out what's going to happen, feeling the pressure of having to remember something really important, but not really knowing what to expect. While they're trying to figure out how to memorize what the teacher is saying, they suddenly realize the instructions have already been given and they're going to look stupid—*again*.

How to Help: Unfortunately, it may take a while before we can talk some educators into the idea that it's acceptable to repeat instructions at least one more time, especially if the listener is genuinely paying attention. Meanwhile, you can help your global learner by encouraging him/her to ask the teacher what the instructions will be *about* before they're actually given. At the very least, your global child needs to understand that missing instructions the first time does *not* indicate a lack of intelligence.

Difficulty 3: Justifying or documenting an answer. As a global learner myself, I can still remember agonizing through a math problem with no hope in sight.

Then suddenly, in a blinding flash of insight, the answer *came!* The pride and relief I felt was always short-lived, as the teacher would challenge me to show him *how* I got the answer. Since he didn't buy the blinding-flash-of-insight theory, he assumed I simply copied the answer from someone else. Because global minds operate with *chunks* of information instead of individual pieces, it's difficult for them to turn what they know into a documented, analytical format.

How to Help: It's important to reinforce the globals' sense of intuition and imagination while you're insisting they be accountable for documenting their work. Celebrate the fact that the answer came at all; then help the globals work backward to figure out what the process was.

Concrete Sequential Learners

Difficulty 1: Reading between the lines. Literature, poetry, social studies—all are among the subjects that can pose a bewildering set of questions to CS students. "Why is *The Red Badge of Courage* red?" "What does the poem *Fire and Ice* symbolize?" "Why is our flag red, white, and blue?" If the answers aren't clearly and immediately evident in the assigned material, CSs can find themselves at a standstill. My niece Kelli summed up this predicament in her typical CS manner as she pointed to the pages in her textbook: "Aunt Cindy, how can I read between the lines? There's nothing *there!*"

How to Help: If you want to help your CS learn to read beyond the written word, it will take time and patience on your part. For Kelli, her dad has probably helped her most. He'll sit down and help her define the terms of the questions, then give her some examples. He never lets her feel that her concrete mind is not intelligent enough to get it; he simply starts over as many times as he needs to until the light comes on.

Difficulty 2: Accepting interruptions or changes in routine. Sometimes something as simple as a fire drill, an assembly, or a special event can almost ruin the CS's schoolday. It's not that CSs don't enjoy a variety of activities; it's just that it's difficult to adjust to anything that disrupts the routine they've established. If Monday is library day and they have to skip that library time to go to the assembly, when will they go to the library? The typical random response of "Don't worry. We'll find another time to go" does nothing to reassure the CS.

How to Help: Whenever you can, try to give CSs as much advance notice as possible that their routine is going to change. One of the best ways to keep

CSs feeling secure in spite of schedule alterations is to practice some "what if" scenarios. For example: "Tom, what if you got to school tomorrow and you found out that your classroom was flooded with water?" "Susan, what if you were working in class and suddenly the fire alarm went off?" By talking through some of these situations in advance, you can prepare your CS to deal with contingencies.

Difficulty 3: Accepting exceptions to the rules. Consistency means more to CSs than the rest of us will ever realize. They have a strong internal sense of equity and fairness and will usually be the first to bring inconsistencies to your attention. Unfortunately, this often takes the form of "tattling": "Mrs. Jones! Tommy's using red ink! You said we could use only blue or black ink!" What's fair for one is fair for all, and CSs are bound to make sure that rules stay carefully enforced.

How to Help: It's especially important when dealing with CSs that you're clear about what needs to be accomplished. As long as you can demonstrate to them that the goal is being met, you'll be more successful in getting them to accept the fact that there may be many ways to get there.

Abstract Sequential Learners

Difficulty 1: Finishing assignments during class. The pressure of timed tests or short-term deadlines is probably more stressful for ASs than for any other style. ASs have a logical, systematic bent that simply can't be rushed and still be thorough enough to produce the desired outcome. Though it may seem to some of us that ASs are just dragging their feet and taking more time than necessary, it won't help to insist they hurry. We often find that ASs shut down when they feel overloaded and pressured to finish quickly.

How to Help: It may be difficult to get your AS's teacher to cooperate in giving more time to complete class assignments, but it never hurts to ask. Try to ascertain the purpose of the assignment, and propose that your AS can meet the goal even if it takes more time. If the teacher won't allow extra time, help your AS practice moving quickly through shorter assignments, giving assurance that this will not be judged as his/her best work.

Difficulty 2: Participating in cooperative learning. It's often difficult to convince ASs that working or studying together in a group would be beneficial. ASs tend to assume that the others in the group are there to act as vacuums, sucking information out of them so the rest won't have to do any work. ASs usually work most effectively when they can work independently, so they're not naturally motivated to cooperate in group efforts.

How to Help: If you can demonstrate the benefit of studying cooperatively, your AS may at least give the group process a chance. Be careful to define what the AS's role in the group will be, and emphasize that the purpose of working together is, as much as anything, to learn the *process* of teamwork.

Difficulty 3: Learning or using gimmicks, games, and so on. As a Concrete Random teacher, I found I frustrated my Abstract Sequential students when I insisted they learn the little gimmicks and memory devices instead of just presenting the information first. I was proud of myself for thinking of a great way to remember how to spell *cemetery*.

"When you were little and your mom played with your toes (this little piggy went to market, etc.)," I said, "do you remember what the last little piggy did?"

One student supplied the answer: "Cried wee, wee, wee, all the way home."

I nodded. "That's right. Well, *this* little piggy cried e, e, e, all the way through the *cemetery!*"

An AS student's hand went up, and I called on him.

"I don't understand what a pig would be *doing* in a cemetery," he protested.

I guess he missed the point!

How to Help: Encourage your AS to identify what the gimmick or neumonic device is supposed to help him/her remember. If it's not needed, don't use it.

Abstract Random Learners

Difficulty 1: Socializing too much in class. School is an intensely social experience for ARs. It's difficult to separate spending time with their friends from the learning that is supposed to happen in the classroom. The most meaningful learning that takes place for ARs is what they can share with those they care about most. Unfortunately, this "group learning" leads to comments on the report card such as "Is entirely too sociable during class" or "Needs to learn to focus on the teacher instead of his friends."

How to Help: Encourage your AR to spend time with friends outside of school, doing things that will help *inside* the classroom. For example, have a homework party—closely supervised by a parent. Instead of constantly fighting the ARs need to socialize, channel that need into productive areas that will result in better academic performance.

Difficulty 2: Following detailed instructions. One of the gifts ARs possess is intuition—a general sense of what needs to be done. It's almost contrary to that nature when the teacher insists they follow step-by-step directions to achieve a particular goal. It's particularly frustrating to ARs when the details seem so unimportant to them and yet are a priority to the teacher.

How to Help: Most ARs can succeed in fulfilling even the pickiest of details if they're properly motivated. Remembering that your AR needs to feel that he/she is doing something that will really matter, seek to find and communicate a personal sense of accomplishment. If nothing else, reinforce the fact that missing one or two details may drastically alter the overall results.

Difficulty 3: Feeling that a teacher doesn't like them. While almost all students want to feel loved and accepted by their teachers, many students can function without specifically receiving that reassurance. ARs, however, are utterly dependent on a positive relationship with their teachers in order to succeed in class. Even if social studies was Larry's favorite and best subject last year, this year it could be his worst if he believes the teacher doesn't like him.

How to Help: You may need to help ARs put things in perspective when it comes to how a particular teacher feels about them. For example, Tracy came home devastated that her name was put on the chalkboard because she was causing trouble. Tracy was sure that her teacher hated her now, and things would never be the same. Tracy's mom asked her how many names besides hers were on the board. "Well," Tracy admitted, "about 26." After Tracy and her mom discussed it, Tracy decided that it was just a bad day for her teacher, and she couldn't wait to get to school the next day and take her teacher an apology and cheer-up-I-love-you card!

Concrete Random Learners

Difficulty 1: Following someone else's rules. For most CRs, rules are really just *guidelines.* After all, rules are for people who are too stupid to do the right thing anyway! CRs often mean no disrespect; it's just that *your* rules may not seem all that necessary to *them.* Since it's common to see a list of "classroom rules" at school, it's no wonder that CRs often find themselves at odds with the teacher's system of discipline.

How to Help: Encourage your CR to discover the *reasons* for the teacher's rules. If the two of you can brainstorm together, your CR may begin to see that the rules really do make sense. Admit to the CR that certain rules may be unnecessary for some, but there is the problem of fairness and accountability. Challenge the CR to come up with some solutions that would keep everyone in class accountable within the parameters the teacher has set. (Sometimes, given the choice, the CR will simply shrug and decide it's not worth the effort to fight the rules.)

Difficulty 2: Not being allowed to use their imagination. The world is full of options for CRs, and limiting their choices is one sure way to quickly stir up a lot of conflict. Teachers don't always appreciate the CR's active and creative imagination when they simply want a straightforward assignment. CR responses like "This is dumb!" or "Why do we have to do this anyway?" often provoke accusations of disrespect from the teacher. It doesn't take long for the conflict to escalate to an irreconcilable power struggle.

How to Help: It's important to teach your CR the need to choose battles wisely. This may take a lot of time, patience, and trial-and-error solutions, but try to show your CR that great imagination is often wasted on petty situations.

Difficulty 3: Investing the time and effort to master concepts and tasks. A frequently repeated motto for CRs is "How much is really necessary?" CRs have a natural desire to conquer as much of the unknown as possible. This means they spend little or no time *mastering* concepts before moving on to new and untried territory. Of course, CRs may believe they have a grasp of a particular idea, only to find out they didn't get it right at all. Their impatience with detail and specific instructions may get them into trouble.

How to Help: It's important to get CRs committed to the outcome before you expect them to pay much attention to what it will take to get there. Remember, you can't *make* a CR want what you want, so sometimes you may just have to back off and watch the consequences unfold. For example, you may say to your CR, "Homework is half your grade in math, but you aren't doing any homework. Is a C the *best* you want to get?" If the CR says yes, you're through negotiating. You've made the outcome known, and the CR has decided it's not worth doing the homework. Now the rest is up to him/her.

MANY WAYS OF BEING INTELLIGENT

Taking hold in schools across the nation is a strong movement that uses Howard Gardner's Multiple Intelligences model.[1] As I wrote earlier, Multiple Intelligences is not a learning styles model, but it provides invaluable information on the many ways your child can be intelligent. Many fine educators have written books detailing ways to use the different intelligences for academic success in school, and there wouldn't be room in this chapter to outline all of these methods. Please refer to the annotated bibliography at the back of the book for some of my favorite resources for practical strategies using the intelligences theory.

Remember, school is often not a good measure of how intelligent or capable children are. Some of your children's traits that cause the greatest frustration to you and their teachers may end up being their best skills and abilities during the rest of their lives. I've pointed out just a few of the difficulties each of the learning styles may encounter in a typical school system. But did you notice that each of those problems is frequently caused simply by differences in learning styles? As a matter of fact, each learning style has more *assets* than drawbacks. If you help your children focus on their strengths, you'll be amazed at what they'll be able to accomplish.

Plan of Action

Using a separate sheet of paper for each of your children, write down what you see as his/her greatest success in school. Why do you think he/she is experiencing this success? Write down what you see as his/her greatest challenge in school. Why is this challenging? Talk with your child about what you wrote, emphasizing his/her strengths and how they can be used to meet challenges and overcome limitations.

Chapter Eight

Making Teachers Your Allies

By now you should be convinced that your child is a wonderfully complex and capable individual, possessing many strengths and abilities that may never be recognized or appreciated in school. Uh-oh—school. Your children must spend several years of their lives in a place that's not exactly known for being flexible and understanding when it comes to students who don't conform to the system. What can you do to make sure each of your children will be valued and nurtured? How can you effectively communicate your child's strengths to each teacher? What if your child's teacher truly doesn't care?

Many parents feel they have little control over the system that has been established to offer their children a formal education. The fact is, parents *do* have a great deal of control—but we need to use it wisely and approach our task positively.

After one of my parent seminars recently, one enthusiastic mother was eager to have me autograph a book for someone else. "I'm giving this book to my son's teacher," she explained. "I'm going to tell her she needs to *read* this!"

I winced. "Please," I said, "don't approach his teacher that way. She may *never* read the book!"

I've been a teacher in the public schools, and over the past several years, I've taught and worked with teachers and administrators in both the public and private sectors. As a result of what I've discovered in person as well as from the resources and contacts available to me, I want to assure you that most teachers care very much about their students. They are, by and large, a dedicated group of professionals who are willing to help parents in their efforts to motivate their children to succeed. But teachers have a difficult job description, complicated by the fact that most of them must deal with 20–160 students every day. Understanding learning styles does, in both the short *and* the long run, make a teacher's job easier. It *is* possible for a teacher to integrate many learning style approaches into the same classroom in practical and effective ways. Included in the bibliography at the end of this book are several resources specifically geared toward helping teachers adapt to various student learning styles.

But what happens if your child has a teacher who either doesn't know about or doesn't teach to the different learning styles? How can you tell teachers about this approach without putting them on the defensive or seeming like a know-it-all, interfering parent? I gathered dozens of trusted colleagues in the education field and posed this very question. I asked these teachers to help me give parents some tried-and-true advice for making teachers their allies instead of drawing enemy lines. I listened carefully, tabulated the written results, and the following list of suggestions represent what I believe is the best advice you'll get about communicating effectively with your child's teachers.

GENERAL CONSIDERATIONS

- Always begin by presuming the best, and treat the teacher as an expert. Assume the teacher already knows about learning styles. Take an article, book, or cassette tape and ask the teacher to read it or listen to it and give you his/her opinion.
- Know that teachers become aware of active and interested par-

ents. A teacher will usually make an extra effort to watch out for that parent's child, not because of favoritism but out of a heightened sense of awareness and personal appreciation for the child.

- Understand that with so many children in the classroom, it's difficult for the teacher to recognize and understand each child's personal learning style. Even a teacher who makes a special effort to discover and value different learning styles in the classroom fights an uphill battle with time and curriculum restraints.

- Visit the teacher under ordinary as well as extraordinary circumstances. Often the presence of a parent who comes only under negative circumstances simply puts the teacher on "red alert." Automatically, the teacher feels defensive, and the visit often starts out on a sour note.

- Don't rely solely on the information you get from your child about a particular teacher, since each person sees the world from his/her own perspective. Naturally, your loyalty rests with your child, but do your best to put the situation into perspective before talking to the teacher.

- Resolve to not be intimidated or threatened by the teacher or the school system. As a parent, your voice cannot only be heard but often carries more weight than you could imagine. This is a power you possess for good or evil—use it wisely!

- Keep in mind that a parent who takes the time to listen to both sides of an issue and investigate many alternatives can be a catalyst to constructive change. A parent who simply demands change based on a single incident or narrow view of the situation can sometimes do more harm than good.

BEFORE THE PARENT-TEACHER CONFERENCE

- Avoid phoning the teacher right after school. There are many last-minute details demanding the teacher's attention, and his/her resources may have been seriously depleted during the course of a hectic day. If possible, call in the morning before school and simply leave a message that you would like the teacher to phone you at his/her earliest convenience.

- Visualize parting from the conference with a positive feeling, even if you are seeing the teacher because of a specific problem. Don't imagine a negative ending before you talk through the issue. What's the best thing that could happen?

- Appreciate the fact that the teacher may use a completely different learning style in teaching than your child uses in learning. Be prepared to ask the teacher for suggestions for helping your child stretch his/her style to accommodate and learn from the teacher's.

- Approach the teacher with a light, easy manner; don't begin with negative comments. Be prepared to give some basic facts about your background. It may be helpful for the teacher to know what you do for a living or what educational training you may have.

- Never try to make the teacher feel inferior to you by trying to sound like you know more than he/she does. Your child deals with this teacher on a daily basis; the relationship you develop with the teacher will affect your child much more than it will affect you. Do your best to keep positive feelings between you and the teacher.

- Try to have specific concerns in mind when talking to the teacher about your child—and don't try to deal with all of them in one session. Feel free to discuss as many successes as you want, but don't try to fix all the weaknesses at the same time.

DURING THE PARENT-TEACHER CONFERENCE

- When discussing your child, include in your questions the same four words: "What can I do?" For example, "Jane's learning style is different from your teaching style. I think it's great that she's learning how to deal with many different approaches. I'm wondering, though, what I can do to help her understand the way you teach? What can I do at home that might help her succeed better in your classroom?" Let the teacher know you and your child are taking the responsibility for learning and coping with the classroom demands.

- Recognize that there are practical limitations on what the teacher can do for your child. Try to make it as easy as possible for the teacher to accommodate your child's learning style while still meeting bottom-line outcomes. For example, if you've decided that your child needs to follow a certain system for recording and keeping track of homework, make up the necessary assignment sheets so that the teacher would only need to fill in a couple blanks and sign the bottom.
- Find out what the teacher's expectations are. How does the teacher know the students are doing a good job? How is student work measured or evaluated? You may discover that a particular teacher puts more emphasis on effort than results, or that a teacher gives points for verbal participation in class discussions. Depending on your child's natural learning style strengths, these expectations may be misunderstood. Once you can define them, you can help your child understand and deal with them.
- Start and end the conference with sincere positive statements. Find the best in the situation, and build on those strengths when you find them. For example, can you tell that the teacher is genuinely concerned? Reinforce that by telling him/her how much you appreciate that concern in the first place.

AFTER THE PARENT-TEACHER CONFERENCE

- Jot a quick note of thanks to the teacher, recapping what you discussed in the way of actions you plan to take, etc. Be sure to reemphasize that you'll do your best to provide whatever support is needed.
- Discuss the conference with your child honestly and positively. Don't make it a secret, or your child may feel that you and the teacher are teaming up against him/her. Emphasize the positive aspects that both you and the teacher discussed about your child. Talk about how to use those strengths to overcome

areas of possible weakness. Make sure your son or daughter wants to work on those limitations as much as you do. Unless you can agree on the goal, the methods of reaching it won't do either of you much good.

- Check back in two weeks or so, just to let the teacher know you're following up on any suggestions you have been given. Solicit any additional input or advice the teacher may have at this point.

AN IMPORTANT REMINDER

It's important to recognize, understand, and value many learning style approaches. Since your child is not just one style, a variety of teachers and teaching methods can help develop many learning style strengths. The more variety he/she experiences, the more opportunities your child will have to discover and develop natural style strengths and to use those strengths to cope with difficult academic demands. Instead of resenting a different approach, do your best to help your child understand and value a variety of methods and instruction.

Remember, every teacher is a lesson in learning for your child. By helping children discover and appreciate their teachers' unique styles, you can prepare them to face a world of differences with the confidence of knowing they can use their strengths to cope with almost anything!

IF ALL ELSE FAILS . . .

It's possible that your child's teacher simply isn't going to cooperate with you, and you'll need to take steps to switch to another teacher or even another school. This should be your last resort, but you should not hesitate to take appropriate action if it becomes necessary. The following will give you guidelines for changing your child's situation with a particular teacher or school.

- Remember, there is a chain of command. Start by talking to the teacher first about the situation and how you feel, using the advice given earlier in the chapter. Allow a reasonable time frame—usually between two to four weeks—for change to occur. Significant change is not just a day away. During this time, document your discussions and the steps you've taken with names, dates, and conversations. In both verbal and written form, make a conscious effort to control your temper and emotions. If the teacher doesn't respond in a satisfactory way, move to next level.

- Talk to a school counselor. Brief him/her on the steps you've taken and what has happened (or failed to happen). Ask for advice. If you do not receive an adequate response, move to the next level.
- Meet with the vice principal. Brief him/her on your action during the process so far and what the result has been. Be as specific as possible about your expectations and what it will take to satisfy you. Continue to document your meetings and any actions taken. If you still do not get satisfaction, move to the next level.
- Meet with the principal. Share what you've done and explain your previous meetings to prove that you've followed the chain of command. If you still aren't satisfied with the response, move to the highest level.
- Meet with the school superintendent. Be prepared to leave copies of your notes from the previous meetings, along with a written statement of your expectations. Give the superintendent at least a few days to respond to you, preferably in writing.

If all else fails, you may need to pull your child out of the school or district entirely. It is rare that you would get this far, but you need to know your options. If it's not realistic to send your child to another school and if it's impossible for you to home school, the school district needs to help you find another situation that would be appropriate for your child.

PARENTS, IT'S YOUR CONFERENCE, TOO!

Since each of us views the world from our own perspective, it's important to remember that our own learning styles will greatly influence how we respond to interactions with our children's teachers. Let's take a quick look at some suggestions for each of the Gregorc learning styles that can maximize our parent-teacher conferences.

Dominant Concrete Sequentials

- Set reasonable limits on your expectations for your child. You tend to be a perfectionist; don't let your need for detail spoil any overall success your child may be experiencing.
- Value self-worth apart from accomplishment. Don't be tempted to simply look at your child's test scores and assignments and judge success or failure without taking other elements into account.
- Be sure the teacher realizes you have feelings, too. If you let the conference focus only on the business of grades and accomplishments, you may never really convey how important your child is to you.

Dominant Abstract Sequentials

- Lighten up! If you approach the conference with an all-business attitude, the teacher may be put off from the beginning.
- Despite the fact that ASs tend to learn best by arguing, try to avoid such a tone when discussing your child with the teacher. Remember, the teacher is likely to take your criticism personally, even if you don't mean it that way.
- Try to keep your child's grades in perspective. Remember that the grade itself is usually not an accurate indication of what a student has learned. Strive to get a bigger picture from the teacher.

Dominant Abstract Randoms

- Keep the conference brief, and don't let the conversation get too personal or off track. Your naturally friendly manner will be a plus, but don't get carried away!
- Try to react less emotionally to demands made by the teacher that you believe are rigid, inflexible, or unfeeling. Point out, as logically as possible, how important it is to you that your child feels valued and loved.
- Don't expect an emotional response from every teacher. Remember, some of your child's best teachers may not express their love and appreciation the same way you do.

Dominant Concrete Randoms

- Make a concentrated effort to follow through with the good ideas you and the teacher come up with during the conference. You may have every intention of doing something at the moment, but you need to set up some means of accountability so you and your child will both stick with the decision.
- Be sure you determine how the needs of you or your child will affect others in the classroom or school. Resist the urge to insist on sweeping change; sometimes you'll need to settle for that first, small step!
- You will have more credibility with the teacher over time if you sometimes accept another's idea without always suggesting alternatives. You'll get better results if you use your need for choices and options sparingly!

Most teachers, both in public and private schools, care very much about the children they teach. Always assume the best about your children's teachers, because that means you *and* the teachers want your children to be successful. You'll quickly become allies working toward the same goals.

Plan of Action

The appendixes at the back of the book contain quick, informal profiles you can use to help describe your child to his/her teachers. There are no formal labels, but the statements and choices will provide a good starting point for discussion between you and your child, and between both of you and the teachers. Preschool and standard profiles are available. I encourage you to use these profiles as practical tools for getting a handle on each child's learning style strengths.

Chapter Nine

They Can't *All* Have ADD!

Not long ago, I attended a half-day workshop designed for parents whose children had been diagnosed with attention deficit disorder (ADD). The seminar was conducted by a reputable pediatrician who was considered an expert on ADD and related disorders, and I was curious to see what parents were being told by the medical community. About 50 parents attended, mostly as couples. I watched as they walked into the sterile conference room and sat down on cold, hard folding chairs that were placed in straight rows. Their expressions ranged from fear to frustration, and they waited nervously for the doctor to begin the instruction they so desperately hoped would give them the solution to their children's behavior problems.

As the doctor began his lecture, he immediately informed us that ADD was considered a genetic problem, and the chances were great that we as parents suffered from at least some of the same symptoms ourselves. I saw several people elbowing their spouses, implying that their child must have inherited this malady from *their* side of the family. The doctor continued by stating that ADD could not be cured, and our children would struggle with this problem for the rest of their lives. I noted the despair that crossed the faces of most of the parents.

As the lecture continued, we sat stiffly in the uncomfortable chairs, watching as the doctor kept putting overhead transparencies on the screen that outlined the symptoms for those who suffered with ADD. I tried to focus on what he was saying, but I couldn't help noticing that I wasn't the only one in the room who was fighting boredom and restlessness. My biggest advantage was that I didn't have a child diagnosed with ADD. The other parents were too worried about their children to allow themselves to admit they were struggling to follow the doctor's detailed lecture.

As he displayed the list of symptoms for those suffering from ADD, I was struck by how many of them fit my learning style. In fact, my visual, kinesthetic, global, Concrete Random characteristics appeared throughout the list. Interestingly enough, the list of ADD symptoms also bore a strong resemblance to the list of qualifying traits for the *gifted* program in many school districts. I noticed many of the parents had recognized their own characteristics showing up on those lists, too, and they began to squirm uncomfortably.

As we sat for almost two hours without a break, listening to a basically monotone lecture, I couldn't help wondering why we were so surprised that children exhibit signs of boredom and attention deficit in the classroom. After all, the doctor himself had told us we were probably just as ADD as our children. Wasn't he aware of how difficult it was for *us* to sit still and listen while he lectured so relentlessly?

Throughout the four-hour presentation, I kept waiting for the moment when someone would get up and give us the *good* news. Amid all these depressing descriptions of our children's shortcomings, when would we find out what was *good* about them? I wanted to get up and tell those anxious parents about another perspective. I wanted to say, "Hey—I know your child is driving you crazy. I know the teachers are disgusted, you're frustrated, and your child is getting further and further behind in school. But the bottom line is this: *YOU'VE GOT A GREAT KID!* Every child has gifts and abilities, and we just have to help you find out how to bring out the best in each one. These children *can* succeed, even if they don't fit the traditional mold. It might be pretty inconvenient for us as parents and teachers to deal with, but there are many methods of transportation for getting our children to the same destination." But no one stood up and even *mentioned* anything positive, and at the end of the seminar I watched as the parents literally trudged out the door, despair written all over their faces.

If you're the parent of a child who has been diagnosed with attention deficit disorder, you've probably spent an incredible amount of time and effort trying to discover how you can best help that child succeed in an educational system that just doesn't fit. You've watched as this bright, capable, spirited child has struggled to concentrate and has become less and less motivated to turn in assignments or study for tests. You've dealt with the frustration of that child continually failing to follow directions and consistently showing a disregard for organization and schedules. You may have turned to both educational and medical professionals for help in identifying and prescribing a remedy so that your child can learn to cope with the discipline and structure of an inflexible and impatient world.

But how do you know which of these professionals will truly recognize the difference between your child's natural learning style strengths and an actual learning disorder? How can you be sure that your child will receive the appropriate diagnosis and treatment?

Even the most competent and understanding professional cannot provide an accurate assessment of your child until you've done your homework. It's unreasonable to expect a physician or educator to know your child better than you do. In an age when the "quick fix" has become an increasingly appealing option, you'll need to take some steps to ensure that you don't allow your child to be labeled or dismissed simply because he/she doesn't fit into the traditional educational mold.

While those in the medical and education professions are dedicated to helping your child learn to successfully cope with the world, you must be sure that the specialists you choose are also dedicated to obtaining a balanced and reasonable view of your child as an individual. How can you be certain that you're doing the best thing for your child? Start with one simple but vital step: *Know your child.*

For example, if you have a child who is a kinesthetic learner, he/she will be in constant motion. The typical kinesthetic learner needs to work in short spurts, not concentrated blocks of time. It's often easier for them to listen while they're doing something else, or to work while they're on the move. There are extremes, of course, but it's important to distinguish how much of your child's inability to concentrate has to do with a legitimate need to keep active.

A child with a more global learning style can often miss the details that a more analytic person focuses on quite naturally. While the global learner usually has a good grasp of the overall concept, it can be frustrating to try and explain analytically what he/she only knows conceptually. Again, it's important that you know how much of your child's failure to remember specific details has to do with the global or analytic bent in his/her learning style.

Please remember I am speaking as an educator and not as a member of the medical profession. For some children, medical intervention may be absolutely necessary. For others, professional counseling may be needed. For many, it will be a combination of professional help while teaching a child coping strategies to deal with tasks that are difficult.

Discipline and structure play an important part in every child's education. But I do believe it's essential that we recognize and appreciate the basic framework and design of each child's mind before we decide that there's a learning disability or attention deficit disorder. I'd like you to consider what I believe are three critical issues related to the diagnosis of and, often, medication for attention deficit disorder.

HOW DO YOU KNOW IT'S REALLY ADD?

Is there a bona fide test to determine a medical diagnosis of ADD or ADHD (attention deficit hyperactivity disorder)? I've spoken to several pediatricians and learning disability specialists. They tell me that even the leading researchers and ADD specialists can't agree on a common definition of ADD, nor can they come to a consensus on the symptoms or treatment. Thomas Armstrong, an outstanding educator and popular author, wrote in a recent article:

> I wonder whether this "disorder" really exists *in* the child at all, or whether, more properly, it exists in the relationships that are present between the child and his/her environment. Unlike other medical disorders, such as diabetes or pneumonia, this is a disorder that pops up in one setting only to disappear in another.[1]

In a related article, several educators asked an even more troubling question:

> After all, there is no definitive test for the disorder and no agreed-upon etiology. There are no blood tests to be run, no x-rays to be taken. It would seem, at least on the surface, that people generally enjoy being told by their physician that they have a clean bill of health and have nothing wrong with them; why, then, do parents wish to come away with a diagnosis of ADD for their child?[2]

Even if parents feel their child is being accurately assessed, how is the distinction made between mild, moderate, and extreme cases of ADD? How can we be sure that ADD is not being overdiagnosed or casually diagnosed if there is no conclusive medical or neurological test? The tests that determine whether or not a child has ADD must, by their very nature, be subjective. As Armstrong pointed out:

> Since these behavior rating scales depend on opinion rather than fact, there are no objective criteria through which to decide *how much* a child is demonstrating symptoms of ADD. What is the difference in terms of hard data, for example, between a child who scores a 5 on being fidgety and a child who scores a 4?
>
> Who is to decide what the final number should be based on? If a teacher places more importance on workbook learning than on hands-on activities, such as building with blocks, the rating may be biased toward academic tasks, yet such an assessment would hardly paint an accurate picture of the child's total experience in school, let alone in life.[3]

If we don't really have an accurate method of diagnosing or treating ADD, why are we often so sure it exists in so many children? What if many of the symptoms of ADD simply point out learning style differences?

WHAT'S WRONG WITH MEDICATION?

Are parents given complete information regarding possible long-term effects of taking Ritalin and similar medications? According to some of the latest statistics, "The production of Ritalin or methylphenidate hydrochlo-ride—the most common medication used to treat ADD—has increased 450% in the past four years, according to the Drug Enforcement Agency."[4] What accounts for this alarming and sudden increase?

Ritalin is classified as a controlled substance. Are parents aware of the risks their children may be taking? The *Physician's Desk Reference* lists one of the contraindications of Ritalin as the onset of Tourette's syndrome (a disorder characterized by uncontrollable motor or verbal movements). That means that if there is any genetic predisposition toward Tourette's, the use of Ritalin could trigger this incurable disease. According to the doctors I've spoken with, there has been a general increase in the incidence of Tourette's syndrome during the past 10 years. Are parents being made aware of this?

Perhaps my greatest concern lies in the message we send to children when we are too quick or casual in prescribing medication to help them succeed. How are we teaching our children to cope with what's hard for them? Are we simply encouraging them to use mind-altering drugs as a method of dealing with difficult situations, or are we also teaching them strategies for working through their problems? Later in life, when they run into trouble again, why are we surprised that the first thing many of our children think about is turn-ing to drugs?

HOW DO WE DEFINE "NORMAL"?

You've surely noticed by now that not everyone learns in the same way. There are so *many* ways of being smart, so *many* routes to take to reach the same destination. If you have a child who isn't experiencing success in school, don't assume it's exclusively your child's fault. After all, who decided that the only way to learn was to sit in straight rows, or listen to a teacher lecture, or concentrate quietly for long periods of time?

Let's encourage that highly active child to find ways of incorporating move-ment without distracting others around him/her. For example, we can teach a child to tap his/her foot without making any noise or to squeeze a rubber ball quietly while listening. Let's teach that global child some methods of turn-ing general knowledge into specific answers on a test. Sometimes something as simple as giving several practice tests or sample questions can really help the global mind to focus on the specifics that need to be recalled on a formal exam. These coping strategies may not be the only solution for a child's learning difficulties, but they must be an integral part of any approach to improve his/her *ability* to learn.

I struggled in college to maintain a B average without having to do many boring or difficult things. When I sat in math or science classes, my mind easily strayed from the subject at hand. The homework and reading from all my college courses were overwhelming, and I often felt as if I were drowning. As I did my homework, I quickly found I was prone to distraction. At the slightest provocation, I took the opportunity to stop working and do something else. As I listened to a boring professor drone on, I usually tuned out, later finding that the information I had missed came back to haunt me at exam time. I was almost always restless, preferring to work in short spurts with frequent breaks. My level of concentration was never intense or prolonged, and I found myself regularly working on several projects at once rather than finishing one at a time. Although I could easily have been labeled as having ADHD, I didn't have it then, and I don't have it now.

You see, the interesting thing is, I found that I love to learn about everything that has to do with what interests me. I was passionately committed to becoming the best English teacher I could be, and throughout my college years and even during my graduate education, I excelled in anything that furthered my goals. I wasn't interested in expending energy to do what didn't interest or compel me. I quickly learned which hoops must be jumped through and which red tape must be cut, and I forced myself to do what was necessary to achieve my goals. I did only what was absolutely essential to get by in the subjects that had nothing to do with my life plan. My more analytic friends were horrified that I felt no remorse at getting C's or even an occasional D as long as my overall grade point average survived.

Not every child who shares my learning style will share my motivation and commitment to a goal. Even with my level of determination, I'm honestly not sure how I would have reacted if my parents and teachers had insisted I had a medical problem or learning disability. If someone had pointed out to me how unlikely a candidate I was to finish formal education and excel in my field, I'm not sure my strong-willed nature would have surrendered to their diagnosis. But what if I weren't so focused on the prize? What if I weren't really sure of what I wanted to do? Some serious self-doubt could have arisen and possibly even crippled me emotionally if I was repeatedly told I had something inherently wrong with me.

NO QUICK FIXES

There are no simple solutions when it comes to the diagnosis and treatment of learning disabilities, especially attention deficit disorder. As a parent, you should do your best to make sure your child has competent medical care and is getting an excellent education. You may have to make some difficult decisions regarding intervention and medication. You may feel defensive and frustrated when you seem to be judged by other parents who don't share your views. But remember, every child is an individual. If you've done your homework and taken the time to really know your child, you can use that knowledge to help your child become the successful learner he/she was meant to be.

When I take my children to the shoe store, the first shoes we try on may not fit. Do I change the foot or change the shoe? Of course, my children must learn to wear shoes; I can't just send them out into the world barefoot. But I must find the shoes that match the design of their feet instead of insisting that their feet conform to the design of a specific shoe. It has been my experience that when my children find shoes that fit, they wear them.

Plan of Action

If your child is struggling in school and an educator has suggested that you have your child tested for ADD, ask for a written description of the disorder and a list of the symptoms. After reading the material carefully, put a check mark by each item that you believe may be explained by your child's learning style needs. When you finish, go back and see how many items you *didn't* mark. Take your edited list to the school counselor or a trusted physician and ask what he/she thinks you're dealing with.

Chapter Ten

Celebrate Each Child!

Most police officers will tell you that movies and television shows about cops usually bear little resemblance
to real life. During my six years as a police officer,
however, there was one undercover investigation that played out exactly as if
we were in the movies.

This assignment concerned jewel thieves and a local jeweler who was a
victim in the theft of almost a million dollars' worth of uncut Australian opals.
The setup was fairly simple. Our informant, a buyer, had been offered some
Australian opals by a seller of questionable reputation. The informant
arranged a meeting with the seller at a large hotel café. Posing as our victim's
dining companions, another detective and I sat with him at a table where we
could see the informant's business being conducted. Other law enforcement
officers were scattered throughout the room playing various roles so our seller
would believe it was simply business as usual.

When the seller took out his briefcase to show the opals, our victim got up and walked by that table, supposedly on his way to the rest room. We waited for a nod of his head to indicate that those were indeed his opals. When he nodded, we brought the scene to a swift and successful conclusion, arresting the perpetrator and bringing him to the police station.

As we were cataloging the evidence, I asked the sergeant if I could open the briefcase that contained the valuable jewels. *After all,* I thought, *when will I ever be able to hold a million dollars' worth of jewels in my hands again?* The jeweler watched as I eagerly opened the briefcase—only to find ordinary-looking stones.

"These are just rocks!" I exclaimed, certain we had been ripped off by someone who had substituted gravel from a driveway.

The jeweler's face registered unbelief mixed with exasperation for my inexperience. "I traveled thousands of miles to own those particular stones," he explained. "They belong to me, and I'd recognize them anywhere."

Over the next two weeks, with the help of search warrants, we found several safe-deposit boxes in which the jewel thieves had stashed hundreds of unset stones. I was amazed at the variety even within each gem family. We separated the gems by color, and when they were spread on the squad room table, free from any setting, many looked identical. Each jeweler took his/her turn sitting at the table so that individual stones could be identified and returned to their rightful owner.

I was doubtful. How could anyone search through these piles of similar stones and know for sure which ones belonged and which ones didn't? I watched as one of our local jewelers sat down and began sifting through one of the piles with a thoughtful expression on his face.

"No, this one's a stranger," he would say. Then he would pick up an identical stone and smile. "Ah, here's a friend. I remember the night I couldn't sleep because I was worried about my wife's illness. I got up at two in the morning and cut this one. See this light angle here?"

I sat in amazement as the jewelers gently and carefully reclaimed the gems that belonged to them.

As parents, we know that each of our children is a unique and precious jewel, regardless of how similar the exteriors may seem. We need to know our children as well as the jewelers knew their stones. In this book, I've offered practical ways to help you uncover your children's strengths and gifts—many you probably didn't realize were there. The next step is for us to remain focused on these strengths and gifts, because we can't build anything positive by highlighting perceived weaknesses.

Dr. Kathy Koch, in Fort Worth, Texas, has an organization called Celebrate Kids.[1] Her philosophy is that children should be celebrated for who they *are*, not just for the special days or events in their lives. It's easy to celebrate birthdays and holidays, but often we get too busy with day-to-day duties to remember to celebrate the *child*. I'd like to give you a few ideas for celebrating your children's strengths, using their natural learning styles. Practice keeping your focus on what your children do *well*, and you may be surprised at how naturally those strengths will start to overcome limitations.

WAYS TO CELEBRATE YOUR CHILD

Auditory Learners

- Help them make lists of words they like the sound of—for example, sarsaparilla, ratchet, Macadamia, Zimbabwe, and so on. Encourage them to use these words in sentences, riddles, or songs. Help them look for new words to keep adding to their lists.
- Let them surround themselves with appealing sounds (you may need to provide headsets!). Encourage them to find the music that seems to provide the best atmosphere for concentrating and working.
- Encourage them to listen to their favorite books on tape, or correlate stories with soundtracks. Point out how much sound enhances the way they remember stories.

Visual Learners

- Let them have colorful, stimulating materials and toys. Encourage them to use things that are visually appealing to help them get and stay organized in a way that makes sense and is comfortable for them.
- Challenge them to use colored pencils or ink in a way that helps what they're writing become clearer and easier to understand. Using a variety of colors can provide a welcome relief from tedious writing tasks.

- Provide as many pictures as possible for the scrapbooks that will someday chronicle their lives. Keep their childhood history books full of photographs and visual images that will capture the best parts of growing up.

Kinesthetic Learners

- Help them find as many ways as possible to keep moving in any given situation without causing disruption or misbehaving. Make it a game to come up with creative ways to use their need for movement.
- Design activities that use up as much energy as they can muster. Let them run errands, walk the dog, and deliver the paper. And don't forget to tell them how much you appreciate the steps they're saving you!
- Watch for careers that call for a lot of movement and energy. Point out the advantages of being able to stay on the move and still accomplish the task at hand.

Analytic Learners

- Ask them to help you establish short- and long-term goals for the family. Let them start the discussion with an outline of the goals they created, knowing that they'll be the starting point for a finished product used by the whole family.
- Ask for their help in figuring out what is needed to accomplish an important goal. Remember to praise their ability to sort through the details and focus on key issues and to fine-tune ideas and concepts.
- Let them help organize the family for a particular project or event. Value their ability to identify and utilize each person's skills.

Global Learners

- Let them tell you their favorite stories in their own words, feeling free to embellish by adding their own personal flair. Praise their use of imagination and creativity.
- Ask them to help you find ways to put what they're learning into action. For example, try applying a math concept to the purchase of refreshments for a slumber party.

- Help them use consensus when making a family decision. Let them know you value their ability to include all participants in the discussion.

Those High in Linguistic Intelligence

- Encourage them to use word games, including crosswords, acrostics, and so on. Let them make up their own word games, especially when creating projects around the house.
- Let them write the family's memory book, recording important observations and choosing the means of recording them (e.g., poems, videos, stories, or plays).
- Help them organize and direct a family holiday production, or let them create the message you leave on your answering machine.

Those High in Logical-Mathematical Intelligence

- Let them help you figure out the best value for products purchased, both day-to-day (such as groceries) and major purchases (such as stereos and automobiles).
- Encourage them to compute the gas mileage and the value of various transportation options on your family trip.
- Present them with challenging problems to solve that will benefit the ones they love most—for example, distributing the family chores or scheduling a particularly busy week.

Those High in Spatial Intelligence

- Encourage them to design graphs or charts to illustrate or convince the family to take action on particular projects.
- Let them play with a variety of picture games (e.g., finding the hidden object or unscrambling words).
- Encourage them to draw or doodle. Help them put their dreams on paper or paint their thoughts on canvas.

Those High in Musical Intelligence

- Challenge them to find the best background music for their various tasks (such as homework or mowing the lawn).
- Help them identify and try various musical instruments. Make

the lessons and practice fun. If they decide they don't like the instruments they've chosen, let them move on to something else.

- Let them choose at least one favorite professional musical event or concert to attend each year.

Those High in Bodily-Kinesthetic Intelligence

- Encourage "tinkering" with various projects, giving them as many hands-on experiences as possible.
- Offer gymnastics, dance, and athletic sports as early as they start showing interest.
- Praise athletic ability with or without high academic grades. Remember, their bodily-kinesthetic strengths may develop into a full-time job when they're adults!

Those High in Interpersonal Intelligence

- Give them the job of monitoring family morale and developing ideas to make everyone feel happier.
- Make them the official "encourager." Provide them with blank cards or small gifts they can choose to give to anyone who needs a lift.
- Give them lots of opportunities to entertain or work with their friends, especially when it comes to doing difficult or boring tasks.

Those High in Intrapersonal Intelligence

- Provide time and space for personal reflection and independent work.
- Encourage them to keep a journal or diary. Ensure protection from unwelcome readers.
- Give plenty of time for making decisions, especially when they involve a change of routines or comfortable methods.

Dominant Concrete Sequential Learners

- Let them help you design and implement a general family schedule or routine. Challenge them to design a format that allows for interruptions or last-minute changes without too much stress.

- Encourage them to keep track of what needs to be done during the coming weeks or months. Challenge them to remind family members of their duties in the most positive and motivating ways.
- Offer rewards for completed checklists and chores. Be specific with your praise and consistent with the consequences.

Dominant Abstract Sequential Learners

- Challenge them to find ways to constructively analyze and improve household systems or chores. Praise them for their insight and thoughtful analyses.
- Encourage them to plan ahead to allow as much time as possible to complete projects and assignments. Give them extra time to deliberate, and don't rush them unless it's absolutely necessary.
- Reward them for their efforts to meet others' expectations by letting them set and meet their own as much as possible. Since they thrive on independence, find as many ways of letting them be on their own as you can.

Dominant Abstract Random Learners

- Give them a weekly or monthly budget of time and/or money to be spent finding ways to encourage others. Value their ability to discover what people need, and help them find even little ways to meet those needs.
- Every day, find a reason to compliment them or praise them—but make your observations genuine and sincere. Remember, "No news is good news" is definitely not an AR motto!
- At the end of the day, debrief your ARs in an informal and loving way, such as over a cup of hot chocolate or a glass of milk. Ask them how they feel about their day and what you can do to help them feel better.

Dominant Concrete Random Learners

- Help them find ways to keep their day moving and full of variety. For example, whenever possible, encourage them to schedule some of their most interesting activities during the times of day that are usually the most boring.

- Challenge them to design new methods for achieving old goals, such as doing chores, taking tests, or listening quietly. As long as they demonstrate bottom-line accountability, praise them for their ingenuity!

- Ask them for their input into as many family decisions as possible, respecting their ideas—and politely declining the ones you can't live with. Let them know they're a vital part of the family and you value their participation.

YOU'VE GOT A GREAT KID!

Have you ever stopped to consider that the very traits and characteristics that annoy you most about your children may actually be the ones that may make them most successful later? If you'll start taking time to celebrate the differences between you and your children, you'll discover that your whole perspective on life may improve more than you ever thought possible!

Our children represent what we hope is our most valuable contribution to the future. What are we contributing to *them?* As you invest your love, time, and energy, consider how much that investment will grow when you nurture each child according to the way he/she is naturally bent to learn. What better retirement plan could we hope for than to see our children mature, take their places in the world, and fulfill their unique potential.

Plan of Action

Using a separate sheet of paper for each child, make a list of at least two ways you can celebrate his/her learning style strengths before the week is over.

Epilogue

Now What?

You've got style! I've got style! All God's children have got
style! And you can't wait to share this with your family, friends,
and colleagues. Great! Keep that enthusiasm! But before you get *too* carried
away, consider the following comments and suggestions.

1. Resist the temptation to "test" everyone and categorize them according to a particular learning style label. Remember, there are *many*
   pieces to the puzzle. The greatest value of learning styles lies in their
   diversity. Don't make them seem like a prepackaged deal.

2. Identify and reinforce the *positive* aspects of a person's learning style
   before you try to change behaviors or perspectives. Avoid such negative references as "Well, what do you expect from a *sequential!"*
   Instead, make a concentrated effort to focus on the positive: "I can certainly see why your global, big-picture strengths are a real asset here!"

3. Although the learning styles theory is sound and the strategies in this book are practical, you can't always expect instant change as you implement these good ideas. Give yourself some time to observe and practice, and you'll be amazed at the difference it will make!

4. Keeping in mind that everyone will view this "learning styles thing" through their own style "screen," be sure you're practicing what you preach as you work to convince others of the importance of this approach. For example, when you're talking with:

Analytics and/or Sequentials

- Establish the credibility of learning styles research and have a list of resources and a bibliography available.
- Be as logical as possible when explaining what learning styles are and why an understanding of them can be so effective.
- Be prepared to share specific examples that demonstrate how understanding and using learning styles has made a difference in your life.
- Value each individual's learning style; do not press to "convert."
- Emphasize that *outcomes* will not be sacrificed by varying methods—bottom-line accountability always stays intact.
- Reinforce that everyone can become responsible for his/her own learning by discovering and utilizing learning style strengths.

Globals and/or Randoms

- Point out how learning styles can boost self-esteem and confidence in one's ability to succeed.
- Validate the strengths of each person's dominant learning style; don't press them to "convert" to a more traditional or analytic approach.
- Value flexibility; emphasize the importance of using many different routes to get to the same destination.
- Remind them how many ways there are of being intelligent. Even those who don't succeed in traditional classrooms can

achieve incredible success later if they understand what they
do well naturally.

As you contemplate the often-daunting task of altering attitudes and transforming systems of education and learning, don't give up! Change may come
slowly, but it will be parents and educators like you who will make more of a
difference for your children than you could ever imagine. Each child is a
complex and wonderful individual. As we're entrusted with their care, let us
constantly strive to find ways to help them discover and use their natural
learning style strengths to find success and make their unique contributions
to the world. As parents, we have no more important task than loving our children. Let us invest our time and effort in developing those strategies that will
truly bring out the best in each child.

The appendixes that follow this chapter contain valuable information and
resources as you continue your journey of knowledge and application of learning styles. Appendix A has a *Plan of Action* form. Ideally, you should fill this
out as soon as you finish reading this book. It will help you summarize and
crystallize what you've learned. Appendixes B.1, B.2, and B.3 contain examples of informal *Learning Styles Profiles*—specifically, the standard school
profile, a preschool version, and an individual profile.

Appendix A

Plan of Action

Date_____

1. As a result of reading this book, list three insights you have had about your own learning style.

2. List three things you have discovered about the learning styles of your spouse and/or children.

3. What are two goals you have for immediate change?

4. What are two long-term goals you would like to achieve either as an individual or as a family?

5. How will you know that understanding learning styles has made a difference in your family?

Appendix B.1

Communicating with Your Child's Teacher: A Student Profile (Preschool Version)

The following is based on the information in the book *The Way They Learn* by Cynthia Ulrich Tobias, published by Focus on the Family. It is designed to be a guide for parents in describing each child's strengths and preferences to a teacher. If you send a SASE to Learning Styles Unlimited, Inc., 1911 S.W. Campus Drive, Suite 370, Federal Way, WA 98023, we'll send you a reproducible copy of the following profile. *It is copyright-free in order to allow you to distribute it for personal and small-group or classroom use. It may not be sold or used commercially.*

Remember, you are *not* necessarily asking for special treatment for your child, and you are certainly not suggesting that the teacher or caregiver compromise standards or excuse your child from meeting fundamental academic outcomes. You are sharing what you know about your child and asking the teacher for insights that may aid you in helping your child understand, appreciate, and cope with demands that may or may not match his/her natural learning style.

The following should be filled out by you as you carefully observe and talk to your child.

Child's Name_____

       Date_____

I. Environmental Preferences (How Does He/She Concentrate?)

Seems most alert during which time(s) of day?

_____

When concentrating, even at play, _____(needs, doesn't need) some sort of intake (food or drink)

Seems to be able to concentrate and play best in
_____ (bright, moderate, dim) light

II. Modalities (How Does He/She Remember?)

Is successful most often when he/she can:

_____ repeat words aloud, or turn information into a song or rhyme

_____ see a picture of what is meant, draw or cut out pictures, or use colorful folders, stickers, etc., to organize toys or materials

_____ keep on the move, take frequent breaks, work in spurts of great energy, shift position often

III. Cognitive Style (How Does He/She Interact with Information?)

When listening to information or directions, usually seems to
(choose one)

_____ get the gist of things, understand the main idea

_____ remember specific details, can repeat things word for word

When being read to, often
(choose one)

_____ doesn't mind if the story is abbreviated or paraphrased; tends to prefer stories that hold a great deal of personal interest

_____ wants to hear every word, no variation from the original story, tends to prefer subjects that can increase knowledge

When playing or creating, usually
(choose one)

_____ prefers a variety of projects in process simultaneously; may spread materials out over several different work areas

_____ prefers to complete one project at a time; works best with a structured schedule; needs a clear and efficient work space; needs to break larger projects into manageable parts

IV. Mind Styles™ (How Does He/She Communicate What He/She Knows?)

On a day-to-day basis, prefers
(choose one)

_____ having a parent or teacher provide predictable plans and routines

_____ understanding the purpose for and having time to complete the schedule and routines

_____ knowing and doing what will make everyone else happy

_____ doing what the inspiration of the moment dictates

When it comes to responding to authority figures, seems to especially need
(choose one)

_____ clear and specific rules and expectations

_____ confidence in the ability and position of the authority figure

_____ reassurance of love and personal worth despite making a mistake

_____ to feel that the person in authority respects and seeks input on the issues

Strengths and Preferences

Which of the following are your child's favorite types of free time activities?

(check all that apply)

_____ Blocks
_____ Legos/other construction materials
_____ Puzzles
_____ Computer
_____ Books
_____ Alphabet blocks/manipulative letters
_____ Sandbox
_____ Nature/science activities
_____ Drawing, coloring, creating with art materials
_____ Outdoor play
_____ Sports
_____ Lacing/sewing cards, stringing beads, pegboards
_____ Role-playing or play-acting
_____ Playing with dolls
_____ Other _____

_____

_____

My child's favorite toys _____

_____

_____

Most often, my child prefers to play

(choose one)

_____ alone
_____ with other children
_____ with adults

Summary

Child's Name_____

       Date_____

I would consider the following to be among my child's greatest strengths:

_____

_____

_____

_____

_____

_____

_____

_____

_____

I feel my child needs encouragement in the following areas:

_____

_____

_____

_____

_____

_____

My goals for my child's school year include:

_____

_____

_____

_____

_____

Here is what I feel is most important for you as a teacher to know about my child:

_____

_____

_____

_____

Appendix B.2

Communicating with Your Child's Teacher: A Student Profile

The following is based on the information in the book *The Way They Learn* by Cynthia Ulrich Tobias, published by Focus on the Family. It is designed to be a guide for parents in describing each child's strengths and preferences to a teacher. If you send a SASE to Learning Styles Unlimited, Inc., 1911 S.W. Campus Drive, Suite 370, Federal Way, WA 98023, we'll send you a reproducible copy of the following profile. *It is copyright-free in order to allow you to distribute it for personal and small-group or classroom use. It may not be sold or used commercially.*

Remember, you are *not* necessarily asking for special treatment for your child, and you are certainly not suggesting that the teacher compromise standards or excuse your child from meeting fundamental academic outcomes. You are sharing what you know about your child and asking the teacher for insights that may aid you in helping your child understand, appreciate, and cope with demands in the classroom that may or may not match his/her natural learning style.

The following should, whenever possible, be filled out by you and your child *together!*

Child's Name_____

       Date_____

I. Environmental Preferences (How Does He/She Concentrate?)

Seems most alert during which time(s) of day?

_____

When doing his/her best work, _____(needs, doesn't
need) some sort of intake (food or drink)

Seems to be able to concentrate and play best in
_____ (bright, moderate, dim) light

Is almost always most comfortable doing homework

_____

(at a desk, on the floor, on the bed, or other)

II. Modalities (How Does He/She Remember?)

Is successful most often when he/she can:

_____ repeat the words aloud, drill verbally, or turn the information
into a song or rhyme

_____ see a picture of what is meant, sketch out an idea, or use colorful folders to organize materials

_____ keep on the move, take frequent breaks, work in spurts of
great energy, shift position often

III. Cognitive Style (How Does He/She Interact with Information?)

When listening to information or directions, usually seems to
(choose one)

_____ get the gist of things, understand the main idea

_____ remember specific details, can repeat things word for word

When reading, often
(choose one)

_____ reads quickly, skipping unfamiliar words or substituting words; tends to choose subjects of personal interest and fiction

_____ reads slowly and deliberately, reads every word, stopping when there is an unfamiliar word; tends to choose subjects that can further knowledge, not much light reading

When organizing, usually
(choose one)

_____ works with piles instead of files; may spread materials out over several work areas; tends to procrastinate

_____ works best with a structured schedule; needs a clear and efficient work space; needs to break larger projects into manageable parts

IV. Mind Styles™ (How Does He/She Communicate What He/She Knows?)

When learning, is
(choose one)

_____ more interested in obvious facts than in hidden meanings

_____ often interested in where a person *got* the facts

_____ most interested in the background of the person *giving* the facts

_____ mostly just interested in how much of the facts are really necessary

On a day-to-day basis, prefers
(choose one)

_____ having a parent or teacher provide predictable plans and routines

_____ designing his/her *own* schedules or routines

_____ knowing what will make everyone else happy

_____ doing whatever the inspiration of the moment dictates

When it comes to responding to authority figures, seems to especially need
(choose one)

_____ clear and specific rules and expectations

_____ logical reasons for procedures and guidelines

_____ reassurance of personal worth despite making a mistake

_____ to feel the mutual respect of the person in authority and input on the issues

Summary

Child's Name_____

Date_____

Here is what I feel is most important for you as a teacher to know about my child:

_____

_____

_____

_____

_____

_____

_____

_____

_____

_____

_____

_____

_____

_____

_____

_____

_____

_____

Appendix B.3

An Individual Profile

The following is based on the information in the book *The Way We Work* by Cynthia Ulrich Tobias, published by Focus on the Family. It is designed to be a guide for describing your individual strengths and preferences to those with whom you live and work. If you send a SASE to Learning Styles Unlimited, Inc., 1911 S.W. Campus Drive, Suite 370, Federal Way, WA 98023, we'll send you a reproducible copy of the following profile. *It is copyright-free in order to allow you to distribute it for personal and small-group or classroom use. It may not be sold or used commercially.*

Remember, you are *not* using this to provide an excuse for not doing what is difficult or unpleasant. You are simply sharing what you know about your own style and providing insights that can help your family and colleagues understand and communicate with you more effectively.

After you have filled out one of these profiles for yourself, try asking another person who knows you well to fill one out on your behalf. It will be interesting to see if the two match!

Name_____

Date_____

I. Environmental Preferences (How Do I Concentrate?)

I am usually most alert during which time(s) of day?

_____

When doing my best work, I _____(need, don't need) some sort of intake (food or drink).

I normally concentrate best in _____(bright, moderate, dim) light.

I'm almost always most comfortable doing work

_____.

(at a desk, on the floor, on the couch, or other)

II. Modalities (How Do I Remember?)

I'm successful most often when I can:

_____ use others as a sounding board to talk through issues or plans.

_____ see a picture of what is meant, sketch out an idea, or use color-ful folders to organize materials.

_____ keep on the move, take frequent breaks, work in spurts of great energy, shift position often.

III. Cognitive Style (How Do I Interact with Information?)

When listening to information or directions, I usually seem to
(choose one)

_____ get the gist of things, understand the main idea.

_____ remember specific details, repeat things word for word.

When reading, I often
(choose one)

_____ read quickly, skipping unfamiliar words or substituting words; tend to choose subjects of personal interest and fiction.

_____ read slowly and deliberately, read every word, stopping when there is an unfamiliar word; tend to choose subjects that can further knowledge, not much light reading.

When organizing, I usually
(choose one)

_____ work with piles instead of files; may spread materials over several work areas; tend to procrastinate until the last minute.

_____ work best with a structured schedule; need a clear and efficient work space; need to break larger projects into manageable parts.

IV. Mind Styles™ (How Do I Communicate What I Know?)

When taking in new information, I am
(choose one)

_____ more interested in obvious facts than in hidden meanings.

_____ often more interested in where a person *got* the facts.

_____ most interested in the background of the person *giving* the facts.

_____ mostly interested in how much of the facts are really necessary.

On a day-to-day basis, I prefer
(choose one)

_____ being provided with predictable plans and routines, specific expectations.

_____ designing my *own* schedules or routines, grasping an overall design or structure.

_____ knowing what will keep everyone happy, what will bring harmony and understanding.

_____ doing whatever the inspiration of the moment dictates, keeping lots of action in my day.

When it comes to responding to authority figures, I especially need
(choose one)

_____   clear and specific rules and expectations.

_____   logical reasons for procedures and guidelines.

_____   reassurance of personal worth despite making a mistake.

_____   to feel the mutual respect of the person in authority and input on the issues.

Summary

Name_____

Date_____

Here is what I believe is most important for you to know about me in order to understand and work with me:

_____

_____

_____

_____

_____

_____

_____

_____

_____

_____

_____

_____

_____

_____

_____

_____

_____

_____

Endnotes Book II

Chapter 1

1. Cynthia Ulrich Tobias, *The Way They Learn: How to Discover and Teach to Your Child's Strengths* (Colorado Springs, Colo.: Focus on the Family Publishing, 1994).

Chapter 2

1. Max Lucado, *In the Eye of the Storm* (Dallas: Word, 1991).

2. Cynthia Ulrich Tobias, *The Way They Learn: How to Discover and Teach to Your Child's Strengths* (Colorado Springs, Colo.: Focus on the Family Publishing, 1994).

3. Rita Dunn and Kenneth Dunn, *Teaching Secondary Students Through Their Individual Learning Styles: Practical Approaches for Grades 7–12* (Boston: Allyn and Bacon, 1993); and Dunn, Dunn, and Janet Perrin, *Teaching Young Children Through Their Individual Learning Styles: Practical Approaches for Grades K–12* (New York: St. John's University, 1993).

4. Walter B. Barbe, *Growing Up Learning* (Washington, D.C.: Acropolis Books, 1985).

5. Herman Witkin and Donald R. Goodenough, *Cognitive Styles: Essence and Origins* (New York: International Universities Press, 1981); Witkin, C. A. Moore, Donald R. Goodenough, and P. W. Cox, "Field-Dependent and Field-Independent Cognitive Styles and Their Educational Implications," *Review of Educational Research* 47 (Winter 1977): 1–64.

6. Howard Gardner, *Frames of Mind: The Theory of Multiple Intelligences* (New York: Basic Books, 1983).

7. Anthony F. Gregorc, *An Adult's Guide to Style* (Columbia, Conn.: Gregorc Associates, 1982).

Chapter 3

1. Cynthia Ulrich Tobias, *The Way They Learn: How to Discover and Teach to Your Child's Strengths* (Colorado Springs, Colo.: Focus on the Family Publishing, 1994).

Chapter 4

1. Anthony F. Gregorc, *An Adult's Guide to Style* (Columbia, Conn.: Gregorc Associates 1982).

Chapter 7

1. Howard Gardner, *Frames of Mind: The Theory of Multiple Intelligences* (New York: Basic Books, 1983).

Chapter 9

1. Thomas Armstrong, "ADD: Does It Really Exist?" *Phi Delta Kappan* (Feb. 1996).

2. Richard W. Smelter, Bradley W. Rasch, Jan Fleming, Pat Nazos, and Sharon Barnowski, "Is Attention Deficit Disorder Becoming a Desired Diagnosis?" *Phi Delta Kappan* (Feb. 1996).

3. Armstrong, "ADD: Does It Really Exist?"

4. Ibid.

Chapter 10

1. Kathy Koch and Celebrate Kids, Inc., P.O. Box 136234, Fort Worth, TX 76136; (817) 238-2020.

An Introductory Annotated Bibliography for Parents

Here are some of my favorite and most trusted resources for learning more about learning styles.

Armstrong, Thomas. *In Their Own Way*. New York: St. Martin's Press, 1987.
    The first book of a man who, after being a learning disabilities specialist for 16 years, decided there was really no such thing as a "learning disability." He challenges the traditional way of schooling, and gives hope and practical suggestions for parents who believe their children *can* learn, but must do it in their own way.

Armstrong, Thomas. *The Myth of the A.D.D. Child: 50 Ways to Improve Your Child's Behavior and Attention Span Without Drugs, Labels, or Coercion*. New York: Dutton Books, 1995.
    A former special education teacher, Dr. Armstrong provides 50 practical, positive ways to help the ADD child. His heartfelt and well-researched position is that ADD doesn't exist and that the children who experience behavior and attention problems are healthy human beings with a different style of thinking and learning.

Armstrong, Thomas. *7 Kinds of Smart*. New York: Penguin Books, 1993.
    Armstrong's latest and perhaps most enlightening book. Using Howard Gardner's model of Multiple intelligences, he presents easily understood descriptions of the seven intelligences, as well as a list of 25 ways to help your child develop each one.

Barbe, Walter B. *Growing Up Learning*. Washington, D.C.: Acropolis Books, 1985.
    Although this book is currently out of print, you'll find your trip to the library to read it well worth your while! The former editor of *Highlights Magazine* shares a wealth of information about auditory, visual, and kinesthetic modalities. You'll find age-appropriate checklists and dozens of suggestions for helping your child learn in many different ways.

Breggin, Peter R., and Ginger Ross Breggin. *The War Against Children: How the Drugs, Programs, and Theories of the Psychiatric Establishment Are Threatening America's Children with a Medical "Cure" for Violence*. New York: St. Martin's Press, 1994.

Dr. Breggin is a psychiatrist who has taken a stand against the use of medication for social control of children and their behaviors. He and his wife have written this compelling book, providing a host of alternative measures for fulfilling the genuine and often inconvenient needs of children.

Butler, Kathleen. *It's All in Your Mind: A Student's Guide to Learning Style.* The Learner's Dimension, P.O. Box 6, Columbia, CT 06237, 1988.
Using Anthony Gregorc's model of learning styles, Dr. Butler has written a workbook designed to be used with teenagers who want to identify and learn to use their learning styles to be better students.

Chess, Stella, and Alexander Thomas. *Know Your Child.* New York: Basic Books, 1987.
This volume is packed with evidence (including longitudinal research studies) to prove that children have their own, unique temperaments from the beginning to the end of life. The authors' "goodness of fit" theory has some practical applications to successful parenting.

Dobson, James C. *Parenting Isn't for Cowards.* Waco, Tex.: Word Books, 1987.
As always, Dr. Dobson presents a compelling case for parents to understand and appreciate their children. Full of practical advice and encouragement, this book also supports the idea that parents must know and appreciate their child's individual personality and temperament.

Dunn, Rita, Kenneth Dunn and Gary Price. *Learning Style Inventory* (LSI) for students in grades 3–12, and *Productivity Environmental Preference Survey* (PEPS) for adults.
Direct, self-report instruments based on rank ordering of choices for each of 104 items. Computerized scoring is available from Price Systems, Box 1818, Lawrence, Kansas 66044.

Dunn, Rita and Kenneth Dunn. *Teaching Students through Their Individual Learning Styles.* Reston, Vir.: Prentice-Hall, 1978.
A landmark work launching the idea of learning styles through environmental preferences and multisensory modality approaches. This book is an important resource for parents and teachers alike.

Dunn, Rita. Editor, *Learning Styles Network,* The Center for Learning and Teaching Styles, St. John's University, Jamaica, New York.

The Learning Styles Network publishes a newsletter, an extensive annotated bibliography, and various materials on learning styles—especially suitable for educators.

Gregorc, Anthony F. *An Adult's Guide to Style.* Columbia, Conn.: Gregorc Associates, 1982.
    This is the definitive volume for identifying and understanding Gregorc's model of learning styles. Packed with definitions and examples, this book is an invaluable reference for serious study.

Keirsey, David and Marilyn Bates. *Please Understand Me: Character and Temperament Types.* Del Mar, Calif.: Prometheus, Nemesis, 1978.
    This book provides a fascinating look at personality types and temperaments. You'll discover how your temperament affects your success in relationships, careers, and life in general.

Kroeger, Otto and Janet M. Thuesen. *Type Talk.* New York: Delacorte Press, 1988.
    This is a fun, easy-to-read guide to the Myers-Briggs version of Carl Jung's personality types. Loaded with anecdotes, this book is one you'll find yourself loaning to your friends!

Rusch, Shari Lyn. *Stumbling Blocks to Stepping Stones.* Seattle: Arc Press, 1991.
    This book relates the touching, true story of a little girl growing up with multiple "learning disabilities" who struggled to become successful in spite of a school system that gave little or no help. Full of hope as well as specific suggestions for other children who may be suffering, this book is a valuable resource for parents and teachers.

Swindoll, Charles R. *You and Your Child: A Biblical Guide for Nurturing Confident Children From Infancy to Independence.* Nashville: Thomas Nelson Publishers, 1990.
    Charles Swindoll has written a compelling and eye-opening book for parents who want to instill lasting moral and spiritual values in their children. Using a scriptural perspective, Dr. Swindoll presents a powerful argument in favor of each child's individuality and value.

Tobias, Cynthia Ulrich and Pat Guild. *No Sweat, How to Use Your Learning Style to Be a Better Student.* Seattle: The Teaching Advisory, 1991.
    A handbook for students using the Witkin model for study skills.

Tobias, Cynthia Ulrich. *I Like Your Style!*
A quarterly newsletter filled with practical strategies and up-to-date resources. Published by Learning Styles Unlimited, Inc. Call (253) 862-6200 to subscribe.

Tobias, Cynthia Ulrich. *The Way We Work: A Practical Approach for Dealing with People on the Job.* Colorado Springs, Colo.: Focus on the Family Publishing, 1995.
This is an enlightening and easy-to-read resource for developing more efficient communication with coworkers. It provides a powerful plan for transforming your on-the-job relationships.

Tobias, Cynthia Ulrich with Nick Walker. *"Who's Gonna Make Me?" Effective Strategies for Dealing With the Strong-Willed Child* (video) Seattle: Chuck Snyder & Associates, 1992.
Focusing on the Concrete Random, strong-willed child, this 45-minute video presents practical, hands-on strategies for bringing out the *best* in your strong-willed child. This is one you'll definitely loan to your friends!

Favorite Children's Books

Brown, M.K. *Sally's Room.* New York: Scholastic, Inc., 1992.
Here is an ageless story for any parent who has fought repeated battles over a messy room.

Hazen, Barbara Shook. *Even If I Did Something Awful.* New York: Aladdin, 1992.
This is a story of unconditional love without compromising parental authority. Good for all ages!

Henkes, Kevin. *Chester's Way.* New York: Puffin Books, 1988.
This delightful story shows children how their learning style differences can help them appreciate others for their strengths.

Lester, Helen. *Tacky the Penguin.* Boston: Houghton Mifflin, 1988.
Here is a wonderful story for any child or adult who needs to be reminded that being an individual definitely has its advantages over simply running with the pack.

One of my favorite posters reads:

We have not succeeded in solving all of your problems. The answers we have found only serve to raise a whole new set of questions. In some ways, we feel we are as confused as ever, but we believe we are confused on a higher level and about more important things.

—Author unknown